Editors: Nicolaus Schafhausen, Vanessa Joan Müller and Michael Hirsch
Translation: Steven Lindberg, James Gussen
Design: Miriam Rech, Markus Weisbeck,
Surface Gesellschaft für Gestaltung, Frankfurt am Main
Printing and binding: Druckerei Lembeck, Frankfurt am Main
Logo Design: Richard Massey and Sarah Morris

This publication is published on the occasion of the exhibition "adorno"
at Frankfurter Kunstverein, Oktober 29, 2003 – Januar 4, 2004

ISBN 0-9726806-3-2
ISBN 0-9726806-4-0 (Volume 1)
ISBN 0-9726806-5-9 (Volume 1 + 2)

Lukas & Sternberg
Caroline Schneider
1182 Broadway #1602
New York NY 10001
Linienstraße 159
D-10115 Berlin
mail@lukas-sternberg.com
www.lukas-sternberg.com

funded by the Federal Cultural Foundation

kulturstiftung des bundes

hessische kultur stiftung

This publication is also supported by the City of Frankfurt am Main
and the Georg und Franziska Speyer'sche Hochschulstiftung.

frankfurterkunstverein

Steinernes Haus am Römerberg, Markt 44, D-60311 Frankfurt am Main, www.fkv.de

ADORNO

THE POSSIBILITY OF THE IMPOSSIBLE

LUKAS & STERNBERG

01 Theodor W. Adorno, *Aesthetic Theory*, trans. C. Lenhardt, (London: Routledge & Kegan Paul, 1984), 323.
02 ibid., 47.

PREFACE

Art—for Adorno it meant above all music, then literature, then painting. His writings contain many unspecified references to "the artwork." By contrast, concrete works in the visual arts play a rather subordinate role within the oeuvre of the author of *Aesthetic Theory*. Adorno, moreover, was certainly less concerned with the analysis of existing artistic production than with art's inherent potential within the social system. Art is the aesthetic space of utopia that has not yet been realized elsewhere—it is representative of the Other, of that which has been exempted from the processes of production and reproduction. The hope—central to Adorno's thought—that an alternative to existing relationships can be intimated in art, at least, turns art into a productive blank space. For what art does above all is point out that this "Other," this thing beyond actually existing society, beyond the "administrated world," can exist at all without utopia having been achieved. "Works of art are plenipotentiaries of things beyond the mutilating sway of exchange,"[01] as it is expressed in one passage in *Aesthetic Theory*, and in another: "One of the crucial antinomies of art today is that it wants to be and must be squarely Utopian, as social reality increasingly impedes Utopia, while at the same time it should not be Utopian so as not to be found guilty of administering comfort and illusion."[02]

It seems that art alone possesses the ability to enable us to experience and, even more importantly, to articulate this "beyond." For Adorno, autonomous art represents a foil to a culture industry that dominates everything and the consequent doubling reality, which merely obscures the true circumstances of the world. This presumes, of course, that the artwork can be detached from all the contexts of this culture industry and its mechanisms for exploitation. Art must remain an abstraction, an artifact that is removed from all efforts, whether commercial or institutional, to tailor it. If need be, it must even abandon its status as art and devolve into cognition.

Adorno's vocabulary was a radically modern one that, seen from the perspective of artistic production, joined forces with the postwar avant-garde of its day. The rise of abstraction and indeed the rhetoric of the avant-garde as such, which is always concerned with the overcoming of the existing, with the search for the absolute, are the central motifs of his *Aesthetic Theory*. The nonfigurative aspect of this art that refuses

03 Theodor W. Adorno, *Minima Moralia*, trans. E.F.N. Jephcott, (London: Verso, 2002), 75.

to make unambiguous statements is manifested, Adorno believed, in the aesthetic material taking form in accordance with the objective historical status of external, non-artistic reality. Only an art that radically removes itself from reality in this way or that outdoes real circumstances by means of criticism can create awareness of the true negativity of the world.

For that reason too, the artwork stands for itself—freed from the economic circumstances to which it is ultimately subject, despite all its autonomy, and independent of the institutional framework into which it is integrated. Only in a few passages did Adorno take into account the framework that art needs in order to become effective. Art *exhibitions* hardly interested him at all, because the juxtaposition of various works is incompatible with the idea that every work possesses an implicit claim to represent single-handedly its entire genre. For Adorno, every work aims at the absolute and thus strives to overcome art itself; in *Minima Moralia* he even speaks of "this impulse to self-destruction inherent in works of art" [03] as their innermost striving.

The utopian function of art is its lack of function—precisely in this point lies what is perhaps the radical dissension with large sections of contemporary artistic practice, for—if we take exhibitions like the most recent *Documenta* as a seismograph of contemporary trends—art in particular seems to have become the terrain on which the deficits or even injustices of the political, the social, can be made evident. Art is increasingly conceived as an instrument of making things visible, related to the present day and the concrete circumstances from which society is formed. That makes Adorno's theory of art problematic today because even the rhetoric of outdoing has become a classic formulation for the avant-garde. Art has become institutionalized at every level and become a fixed feature of the social system with contexts of economic exploitation that are expressed increasingly openly. We seem to have lost faith in the utopian power of art to point to a radically other world that is nonetheless only a tiny step away from the existing world.

Vast areas of contemporary art could be accused of giving in to the desire for an unconditional identification of advanced political and social concerns with artistic and aesthetic ones. Much of contemporary art practice seeks to displace the enigmatic character of artworks that Adorno took to be central and make artworks the bearers of a discursive meaning, statement, or position. This kind of pragmatism differs radically from Adorno's thought. One could argue along with Adorno that becoming involved with society in this way ultimately affirms its conditions. On the other hand, a turn to political or social concerns does not necessarily mean a break with art's immanently enigmatic character. Although on the surface the program that Benjamin advocated of resolving art into life or into politics may still seem to be relevant today, in fact it is precisely the character of art as art that gives it its potential to be effective in a way that is still irrevocably different from the quotidian.

The Frankfurter Kunstverein's exhibitions—reflected by past projects with programmatic titles like *Neue Welt* (New world), *non-places*, or *nation*—would surely not have appealed to Adorno. It may therefore come as a surprise that this institution should present an exhibition under the motto *adorno* in the year that marks the hundredth anniversary of his birth. Be that as it may, our concern is not to illustrate Adorno's ideas about art by means of selected artworks, since neither a thesis-like reduction nor visual illustration would do justice to the complexity and radicalness of his instrumentalization of art as the only remaining source of hope in a society that can be best described in its negativity.
This exhibition at the Frankfurter Kunstverein therefore also includes works of contemporary art—that is to say, works created at a time when the visual arts have changed substantially vis-à-vis the positions of advanced postwar art.
Works by Ad Reinhardt, Gustav Metzger, Bruce Nauman, and Gerhard Richter form the chronological starting point of the exhibition; works by Peter Friedl, Henrik Plenge Jakobsen, Markus Schimwald, and Cerith Wyn Evans that were developed specially for the project, sometimes relating directly to Adorno's texts, form its end point. Many of the works obtain their relationship to Adorno's thought only within the context of the exhibition. In that sense, it is more a matter of coming closer to his thought than of providing evidence of its relevance.

Where the first volume of this publication collects essays by various writers from philosophy and cultural studies that probe Adorno's thought with an eye to its relevance today while focusing on his large-scale socio-theoretical models and the microlevels of his writings, the present volume, in addition to presenting the works included in the exhibition, is concerned above all with Adorno's relationship to the visual arts.

We would like to take this opportunity to thank especially the Kulturstiftung des Bundes for its support for the exhibition and the two-volume publication. We are also grateful to the city of Frankfurt am Main for its support. We wish to thank the Hessische Kulturstiftung and the Georg und Franziska Speyer'sche Hochschulstiftung for supporting the publication as well as Art Frankfurt for additional support for the exhibition. Above all, however, we are grateful to the authors and the artists whose works and ideas have made this exhibition possible in the first place.

Vanessa Joan Müller, Nicolaus Schafhausen
September 2003

Translated from the German by Steven Lindberg

01 Theodor W. Adorno, "The Curious Realist: On Siegfried Krakauer," in idem, *Notes to Literature*, trans. Shierry Weber Nicholson, vol. 2 (New York: Columbia Univ. Press, 1992), 58-74, esp. 61 (hereafter cited in the text as CR).

02 André Breton, "Manifeste du surréalisme" (1924), in idem, *Œuvres complètes*, vol. 1 (Paris: Gallimard, 1988), 309-46 (hereafter cited in the text as MS).

03 Theodor W. Adorno, *Aesthetic Theory*, trans. Robert Hullot-Kentor (Minneapolis: Univ. of Minnesota Press, 1997), 53 (hereafter cited in the text as AT).

ADORNO IS AMONG US

Isabelle Graw

1. Blindfolded

Thinking with pencil in hand: Adorno used this image to describe the working method of his mentor and friend, Siegfried Kracauer.[01] A formulation that—it might be remarked in passing—recalls André Breton's characterization of *écriture automatique* as a method of writing that immediately follows the "flow of thoughts."[02] Adorno intended this image as a compliment. It is one of his many metaphors for a mimetic *comportment* that interested and perhaps even fascinated him. If Kracauer thinks, according to Adorno, with pencil in hand, this means that for him thought flows directly, as it were, into the pencil, and that conversely, thought is pulled along by the pencil's movement. This thought is mimetic in the sense that it recapitulates the movements that the hand performs with the pencil. This understanding of mimesis—which does not involve the representation of reality, but a conservation of the mimetic capacity within the artistic process—is one of modernism's most important topoi. It is a topos that pervades the visual arts of the twentieth century, and it is one they often thematized. One need only think of Paul Klee's celebrated statement that the eye pursues the course traced out for it by the work, a kind of modernist credo, with which he styled himself the mere executing agent of a higher order. However, this motto does justice to *one* essential aspect of artistic production: the mimetic impulse. Robert Morris's series of *Blind Drawings* from the 1970s may be understood as a reflection on this myth and its productivity. For the information that the artist produced them blindfolded is immediately taken back in the drawings themselves. Every image contains a text at its bottom edge with indications concerning the procedure used to create it, and yet in the end this text is supposed to be a "lie." The modernist myth is undermined and at the same time rendered productive.

Adorno too regularly expressed his enthusiasm for a particular form of "mimetic procedure," and he described art in general as the "refuge for mimetic comportment": "In art the subject exposes itself, at various levels of autonomy, to its other, separated from it and yet not altogether separated."[03] It is the relationship that appears in art between a gradually autonomous subject and its other, a relationship that Adorno conceives of as mimetic. Adorno breaks with the classical conception of mimesis as imitation. He is concerned with a mimetic behavior that, far from imitating, pursues a

04 Theodor W.Adorno, "Die Kunst und die Künste," in idem, *Gesammelte Schriften*, vol. 10.1 (Frankfurt am Main: Suhrkamp, 1997), 432-52, esp. 448.

course that is traced out for it, as it were, by it itself. And indeed, he was primarily interested in those artists who, he felt, conformed and "clung" to their material and gave themselves over to it. And indeed, for Adorno, Kracauer was more artist than theoretician. Why else would he have described him as a "curious realist" and said of his thought—in a slightly discrediting manner—that it was more contemplation than thought, in other words not theoretical (CR 62)? Kracauer's results appealed to him the more, "the more blindly he immersed himself in the materials his experience brought him" (CR 65–66). We encounter a comparable formulation in the *Aesthetic Theory*: that aesthetic rationality must "plunge blindfolded into the making of the work rather than directing it externally as an act of reflection over the artwork" (AT 115). That appears at first to be a gesture of mystification, which glorifies the artist as the mere executive agency of something that is given objectively and plays off mimetic behavior against "reflection" as if it were a question of polar opposites. But the situation is more complicated than that. First, Adorno conceded repeatedly that art must have "passed through" the subject in order to be art. This means that artworks have definite need of a subject, because their objectivity can only exist as mediated by that subject. Yet after they have passed through this subject, on which they depend, they also leave it behind. Artworks, for Adorno, are the "better subjects," and as useful as it seems to join him in calling attention to the "subjective factor" today, this heightened formulation seems extremely strange. Second, he viewed art as stretched between two poles, that of a "a rational [moment] that establishes unity" and that of "a diffuse, mimetic moment."[04] One might therefore regard the concept of construction as the complementary concept to mimetic behavior. Construction, for Adorno, extends subjective domination and limits it at the same time. Construction is supposed to emerge from the thing itself in a quasi-automatic and necessary manner: "Construction is not the corrective of expression, nor does it serve as its guarantor by fulfilling the need for objectivation; rather, construction must conform to the mimetic impulses without planning" (AT 44). For Adorno, all artworks worth discussing had to display a high degree of this constructedness. Which is something quite different from submission to a predetermined scheme or a system of rules. Adorno always reacted with aversion to that which is stamped or imposed on the artwork from above, a reaction that is

05 Theodor W. Adorno, "The Artist as Deputy," in idem, *Notes to Literature*, trans. Shierry Weber Nicholson, vol. 1 (New York: Columbia Univ. Press, 1991), 98-108, esp. 106.

rooted in his proto-avant-garde attitude, in his fundamental rejection of the conventional and the traditional. The fact that it can actually be productive to quite consciously submit to a given convention, and that artists may have no choice but to refer to certain conventions, which they naturally shape and modify in their turn: these are considerations that run counter to Adorno's conception of the subject. A conception that ultimately turns and grants the subject, especially the "discursively thinking" subject, the sovereignty to elevate itself above its conditions.

What, then, would Adorno have said of an artistic movement like conceptual art, for which the contestation of the idea of the artist-subject was decisive? Assuming one wished to speculate, I think there is reason to suppose that he would probably have responded with alienation to the conceptual practices of the late 1960s, which declared their submission to a system and the elimination of the subject as their program. He would probably have accused them of being nothing more than a mere analogue of the administered world, wholly constructed and strictly objective artworks, which—by dint of their "mimesis of funktional Forms" (AT 58)—tend to become a form of commercial art. From today's perspective, one might object that the "administrative aesthetics" (Benjamin Buchloh) cultivated by conceptual art was a truly artistic phenomenon, whose objectivity was overdrawn and pervaded by irrational elements, and whose "objectives" were radically different from those of the society. Here at the very latest, however, Adorno could unveil his "killer argument," the charge of insufficient "formal elaboration." He was skeptical of any attempt to abandon oneself to the contingent as informal painting did, a gesture that would relieve the artist of the "burden of giving form" (AT 329). An art that pretends to give itself over exclusively to chance did not hold much interest for Adorno. For the artist was for him a guiding director, a subject in conscious command of his material, and as he made clear implicitly in a text on Valéry, the idea that people might become "mere receptive apparatuses" was anything but a goal worth striving for in his view.[05] I think would have been just as disapproving of Breton's ideal of a "recording apparatus" (MS 330). It would have smacked too much of capitulation for him; he would have sensed "aesthetic regression" in it. In view of this, it is all the more astonishing that time and again, Adorno was able to champion and become positively

06 Theodor W. Adorno, "In Memory of Eichendorff," in idem, *Notes to Literature*, vol. 1 (note 5), 55–79, esp. 70 (hereafter cited in the text as IME).

07 Theodor W. Adorno, "Valéry Proust Museum," in idem, *Prisms*, trans. Samuel and Shierry Weber (London: Spearman, 1967), 173–85, esp. 182.

08 Adorno, "Valéry's Deviations," in idem, *Notes to Literature*, vol. 1 (note 5), 137–73, esp. 162.

09 Theodor W. Adorno, "Parataxis: On Hölderlin's Late Poetry," in idem, *Notes to Literature*, vol. 2 (note 1), 109–52, esp. 110.

enthusiastic about the *purely receptive* attitude that "clings" and hews closely to that which is given.

2. The Artist as Intentionless Miner?

There are numerous passages that bear witness to this fascination: from a text on Eichendorff's writing, which Adorno praises for allowing itself to be borne along by the "flow of language"[06] to comparable statements about Proust ("flux of experience"), to a passing comment on action painting and aleatory procedures, of which Adorno writes that the "productive function of surprising moments that are not imagined" cannot be denied (AT 58). Adorno displayed a similar tendency in his reception of Valéry, in which he praised the latter for a method that was effectively his own. With "incomparable authority," he writes, Valéry demonstrated the artwork's objective character, its immanent coherence, and the accidental character of the subject with respect to it.[07] He might have used the same words to describe his own concerns. In Valéry, he saw a precursor and a comrade in arms, a kind of "spiritual brother" who, like him, proclaimed the artist to be the "executive agent" of his material: "Valéry's artist is a miner without light, but the shafts and tunnels of his mine prescribe his movements for him in the darkness,"[08] writes Adorno in a passage that leaves no doubt that he embraces this image of the artist. Should we, then, understand this artist as "a miner without light," as someone who blindly gives himself over to an external determination? Not at all. Essentially, the fact that he works without light only means that he is not guided by an intention. Adorno was no friend of intention, if only because he was convinced that language "overshoots" the author's mere intention. Instead of reducing an aesthetic object to intentions, one should rather investigate to what extent it obeys "the compulsion of the work itself."[09] Thus, his skeptical view of intention was the result of an aesthetic approach that took aim against a subject-centered aesthetics, against an aesthetics that began with subjective experience. By contrast, he wanted to grant priority to the object and did not by any means wish to see it reduced to subjective intentions. Alexander Kluge recounts an anecdote that is revealing in this regard; it illustrates Adorno's "intention phobia" beautifully. Together

[10] Peter Laudenbach with Alexander Kluge, "Nur das unsichtbare Bild zahlt: Alexander Kluge über den Philosophen Adorno, den 11. September und die Flaschenpost der Kritischen Theorie," *Tagespiegel*, 11 September 2003, 25–26.

with others, Kluge was involved in a project to shoot a nine-hour film about the student movement, and according to Kluge, Adorno said that they should film "blind." [10] Only by recording something without intention would he turn something up, and "you will see what that is afterwards." Here again, Adorno gives proof of his conviction that it is the aesthetic object—in this case the student revolt depicted in the film—to which priority is due, because (as he never tired of asserting) it possesses its own lawfulness. And therefore also, one is not permitted to seek to realize intentions in it.

These reservations concerning intentions and the explanations that refer to them run through all of Adorno's aesthetic writings. For example, he dismissed Riegl's concept of the *Kunstwollen*, or artistic will, with the terse remark that what decides about a work is seldom what was intended with it (AT 60). And in his text on Eichendorff, he polemicizes against the "perennial question" of intention, writing that the question is "irrelevant" in the face of the actual composition (IME 74). Intention, then, according to Adorno, is unable to reach what was artistically accomplished. Is it necessary to go this far? The answer, I think, is yes and no. To make productive use today of Adorno's skeptical view of intention means to set limits upon the validity of intention as an "ultimate explanation." It is something else entirely to deny that it has any meaning whatsoever. However, in view of the fact that in portions of the art world an astonishing "intention fixation" currently seems to hold sway—a fixation of interpreters on what was supposedly intended—we might turn to Adorno to call attention to all those aspects that cannot be assimilated to those intentions, or that exceed them. Indeed, precisely in the press statements of art institutions, one regularly encounters claims to the effect that artworks have "intentions" or concerns, as if these were implemented in or by them. This is where the fixation on intention shows its effects. In my view, the tenacity of such explanations based on intention has to do with the fact that they seem to explain art away "convincingly," that is, by reference to the individuality of the artist. It may perhaps be regarded as a consequence of this "intention fixation" for the self-conception of artists that today, many of them find themselves obliged to formulate their concerns in writing in the clearest possible terms and in a manner that often has something self-justifying about it. These are phenomena that are

[11] Marcel Duchamp, "The Creative Act," in idem, *The Writings of Marcel Duchamp* (New York: DaCapo, 1989), 138-40, esp. 139.

rooted in misunderstandings in the reception of conceptual art. What was once the programmatic attempt of conceptual art to demystify art and to reframe it as the sober description of a project (and it must be noted that in retrospect, these "projects" seem abundantly idiosyncratic and leave no doubt about their stylized character) has by now congealed into the dreary convention of declarations of intent that resemble press releases. As if art were a means-end relation, and the artist were a self-transparent subject undertaking the simple artistic "implementation" of his project or plan.

3. No End of Strategy

In fact, Marcel Duchamp had already taken the wind out of the sails of the notion that in art, something intended by the artist is expressed, with his "personal art coefficient." This coefficient—in the words of Duchamp's formula, which flirts with the impression of scientific rigor—is an "arithmetical relation between the unexpressed but intended and the unintentionally expressed."[11] In other words, what is expressed is not necessarily what was intended, and conversely, what is intended generally remains unexpressed. Adorno would surely have been pleased with this drastic statement, especially because it relativizes intention in a way that is tantamount to undermining it. In my view, however, to restrict the scope of intention in this manner need *not* necessarily mean that we must rush to throw the baby out with the bathwater and set aside the image of the artist who works *strategically*, who indeed pursues intentions—an image that arose in the 1980s and took hold in the 1990s—in favor of its "intentionless" counterpart. Even if these two images of the artist—the strategic artist and the intentionless one—might at first glance seem difficult to combine. I would suggest, by contrast, that one further define the idea of "artistic strategy" (an idea that acknowledges the artist's possibilities for action and intervention) by first of all going, entirely in the spirit of Adorno, to the artworks themselves and exploring how they execute strategies, or how strategies are executed in them. In doing so, one would arrive at the conclusion that artistic works are by no means wholly accounted for by these strategies. Moreover, the "strategy" whose expression artworks also are—or *can* be—need not necessarily coincide with what the artist thinks or asserts that (s)he strategically intends.

At the moment when the notion of the artistic subject as master of him- or herself —a notion that is bound up with the concept of artistic strategy—is revealed to be a fiction, it becomes possible to propose a different description of the strategically operating artist. One cannot look to Adorno for assistance in this enterprise, however, because his ideal of the subject is every bit as diametrically opposed to it as is his aforementioned "phobia of intention." After all, he based his ideas on a strong subject, who was not only supposed to be in a position to "cling" to what is given but also had to draw the right consequences from it. Thus, the above-mentioned "miner without light" also had to possess the ability to recognize what the shafts and tunnels prescribe to him or her with seeming objectivity, and then to act according to this "demand."

4. The Problem of Judicial Decree

The fundamental problem of Adorno's aesthetics is its regulative ideas. For example, specific demands are supposed to emanate from the "material" as if they were given in advance. However, this is also the price he pays for his normative aesthetics, which pronounces judgments on the basis of particular assumptions. On the one hand, there is the artist, who is supposed to fulfill an "objective" demand by yielding to mimetic impulses. On the other, there is the mimetically functioning artwork, which finds itself, as it were, or "makes itself like itself": "The mimesis of artworks is their resemblance to themselves" (AT 104). It is not the aim of the artwork, then, to copy the features or behavior of something else, but rather to become similar to itself. This "self" of the artwork, for its part, seems to be given in advance, as if every artwork had its own aesthetic ideal already inscribed within it and had only to comply with it. And the artist would then be the one to whom the only remaining responsibility falls: to see to it that the artwork discovers this path to itself. This is a double fiction, and one that, besides Adorno, only Clement Greenberg has made productive in a comparable manner. In order for it to work, when all is said and done there must be an observer who possesses tremendous authority, because everything hinges on his or her subjective evaluation. Not only must (s)he be fundamentally capable of recapitulation and recognize that "immanent lawfulness." This "immanent recapitulation" (which is construed as a mimetic process) also endows him or her, as it were automatically, with the ability to measure the object against its aesthetic ideal and to decide if that ideal has been achieved. However, the consequences that follow from this postulate of the privileged observer—privileged because endowed with the capacity for mimetic empathy—are not discussed in Adorno's writings. To my knowledge, he hardly reflected on the factors that rendered him capable of this form of "adequate" reception. The figure of "immanent recapitulation" is also problematic insofar as it implies the possibility of unmediated access to and seamless assimilation of the artwork, which of course do not exist in this manner, not least because they ignore the performative contribution of the viewer. The latter's perception, after all, is fundamentally mediated and shot through with projections and misjudgments.

In this scenario, the artist too must be at the summit of his of her work and immediately assimilate the demands that supposedly emanate from it. This leads to the assumption that there is a given "state" of the material, from which it would seem to follow logically that certain approaches fall behind this "state," while others stand level with it. Thus, for Adorno, figurative painting—which presupposes the depiction of the human being and the latter's representability—had definitively reached its end. Today we would say that the problem cannot be figurative painting in general, but rather a certain type of artistic treatment of figurative painting. It is entirely conceivable that one might argue convincingly for the figurative images of Alex Katz while at the same time regarding Lucian Freud's work with skepticism. But in order to think productively about current problems in art theory, it is not at all necessary to go the entire distance and subscribe to Adorno's postulates without reservation. It is equally possible to stop halfway.

5. To Follow Where the Hand Is Drawn

"To follow where the hand is drawn"—for Adorno, that was "mimesis as the fulfillment of objectivity" (AT 115). And objectivity attaches to the direction in which the hand is ostensibly drawn. A direction that is supposedly given in advance. If we bracke

[12] Isabelle Graw, "Der fleckige Boden des Ateliers: Über die neuen Bilder von Christopher Wool," *Texte zur Kunst,* no. 49 (March 2003): 168–71.

out this problem, which is rooted in his normative aesthetics, this postulate stands above all for his *recognition of a mimetic principle* in art, and I would say of this principle that it was long unjustly neglected by art theory. While recent years have seen an increased readiness to acknowledge the immanent lawfulness and "relative autonomy" of art, this concession has largely remained schematic and abstract. No attempt has been made to identify the concrete theater of this immanent lawfulness within the artworks themselves. On the basis of Adorno's thesis of art as the "refuge of mimetic comportment," however, it is possible to specify the juncture where autonomy and heteronomy mesh and intertwine more concretely. This juncture is the mimetic principle, which stands for an idiosyncratic and unpredictable dynamic as well as for the orientation towards an other. The images of Christopher Wool may serve as an example here, because they themselves demonstrate their implication in mimetic, quasi-automatic processes, and at the same time give proof that the decision to use a particular technique—in this case a rudimentary silk screen process—has particular consequences, a dynamic unleashed by the silk screen process itself, which the artist seems merely to obey.[12] At the same time, of course, he opted for this experimental setup, stood at the ready, and made particular provisions to ensure that the process—which he now seems merely to witness—unfolds in a particular direction. Adorno's mimetic conception is very useful for the conversion of this situation into an aesthetics of production. He too took as his premise an artist endowed with the capacity for "passive activity." However, he posited a "strong subject," a notion that has since become questionable. For what at first had smacked of surrender, self-effacement, and the total abandonment of the self to external forces turns out in the end to be dependent on a "strong subject." Thus, Adorno credits Eichendorff with a "suspension of the ego," an ego that supposedly surrenders itself to "something surging up chaotically" from language (IME 65). At the same time, however, the poet must also be "strong" enough to summon the strength for this weakness, to arrive at a weakness that no longer resists the descending flow of language: "that is the descending flow of language, *the direction it flows of its own accord*, but the poet's power is the power to be weak, the power not to resist the descending flow of language rather than the power to control it" (IME 70; my emphasis). Thus, it requires a certain "power" to abandon

13 Isabelle Graw, "Sublime Aneignung: Sherrie Levine," in idem, *Die Bessere Hälfte: Künstlerinnen des 20. und 21. Jahrhunderts* (Cologne: DuMont, 2003), 48–50.

oneself to the direction that Adorno presumes to be given in advance and in which language ostensibly pulls one. Faced with such notions, one might legitimately ask what about them could possibly be relevant to art theory today. Especially because at first glance they remain mired in a subject-object dichotomy. Is it not banal to say that weakness requires a certain strength? Not at all. For even in the context of an artistic practice that seems to be most hostile to the subject, one will sooner or later be forced to concede that the subject left its traces behind in it. The appropriation art of the 1980s is a good example of this, especially because it drew upon the myth of the critique of the subject. It was presumed that the point of such art was not its subjective approach, but the original that was appropriated in any given case. As the name already suggests, art was supposed to be defined in terms of appropriation. However, if one considers the early works of Sherrie Levine—for example, the rephoto graphed Walker Evans photographs that helped to make her one of the most prominent exponents of this practice—it emerges that these works do indeed require a subject, a subject that makes certain decisions, opting for example for a particular type of frame or for an experimental setup that opens the subject and renders it responsive to external phenomena (to that which is to be appropriated).[13] The question, then, of how the subject "enters" seems to me to be worth exploring with respect to the most various forms of artistic practice, from *écriture automatique* to appropriation art. Moreover, Adorno breaks through the rigid confrontation of subject and object with the very conception of art as a mimetic procedure, for it is no longer possible to draw clear boundaries between the artist who "clings" and conforms to his object and that object itself.

6. At the Writing Desk

Why did Adorno decide to revive the Romantic idea that language pulls one in a particular direction as if of its own accord? Alongside his desire to do justice to the aesthetic object, there is, I think, an additional explanation. Here as so often, Adorno ascribed a subjective experience (that of the writer) to the object (language). The person who writes will commonly report an experience in which they feel they are

14 Britta Scholze, *Kunst als Kritik: Adornos Weg aus der Dialektik* (Würzburg: Königshausen & Neumann, 2000), 105.

being pulled along by language as they glide from one sentence to the next. It speaks, it writes, one "is written." From this "subjective feeling," which has phantasmic features, Adorno derived the notion of a native direction of language. Nevertheless, his mimetic postulate is significant for the purposes of an aesthetics of production. For from the perspective of such an aesthetics, it is actually quite relevant that at the outset, the person who writes (or composes) often does not know where their language is leading them. Even the use of outlines does not enable one to rule out this form of unpredictability. Indeed, it is usually characteristic of structural plans that one is continually discarding them and adapting them to changing developments. A new question may surface quite unexpectedly, emerging from considerations that seemed secondary at first. Thus, it may in fact seem to the producer as if it were language itself that were setting the course. Adorno's reader, incidentally, finds him- or herself exposed to a comparable dynamic. In the process of reading Adorno, (s)he has plunged before (s)he knows it into a thought that draws him or her along with it. Adorno makes the reader participate in the process-like character of his thinking. For example, the further ahead one forges through the *Aesthetic Theory*, the more intensely one plunges into his thinking, including its abrupt transitions and leaps. As soon as one has entered upon this reading experience, one already becomes a part of it and becomes the fellow champion of a brand of thought to which paradoxical formulations and aporetic constructions quite simply belong. The reader "reads him- or herself in" and becomes accustomed to the sound, so that formulations that previously seemed alien suddenly appear to be transparent. Mimetic empathy can reach the point of adopting particular mannerisms. Mimetic "clinging" becomes assimilation. And indeed, Adorno's writing has a contagious quality. That he himself worked in a highly "assimilating" manner has recently been pointed out by Britta Scholze, who has aptly described the *Aesthetic Theory* as a "passage through the categories of idealist aesthetics," a passage, moreover, in which Adorno borrowed foreign elements without in every case disclosing that he had done so.[14]

7. Autonomy and Heteronomy

However, to take up these "categories of idealist aesthetics" today also means to brush them against the grain, to beat them like a dusty carpet, which one examines to see if it is still useable at all. For Adorno, to adopt something mimetically was synonymous with taking up a "critical" position against it. Mimesis, for him, possessed a critical function; a critical claim was supposed to be connected with mimetic conformity and "clinging." This reversal of mimesis into critique resembles a magic chain of events, in which the "mimesis of the hardened and the alienated" or the "mimesis of death" is already supposed to be synonymous with "critique." One might counter this hope with the concrete experience of contemporary art, which does not confirm it. On the contrary, it shows that an automatism of this kind can by no means be relied upon to occur. Neither the artistic strategy of affirmation, which was associated during the 1980s with artists like Jeff Koons or Haim Steinbach, nor the much-evoked "techniques of outdoing" are automatically critical. An artwork that carries conditions to extremes is not therefore critical of them—far from it. For example, Sarah Morris's film *Capital* certainly attempts to outdo capitalist conditions. In a sort of "microstudy," it dismantles them and presents them to the viewer. However, it would be going too far to read it as a critique of capitalism for this reason. The idea that an artwork could articulate a critique seems to me, in any event, to be questionable. For precisely where and how is this critique actually supposed to occur? If critique is understood in the conventional sense, as a position that objects to errors and omissions, then artworks are only capable of critique in exceptional cases, for example in Hans Haacke's early works. And here too, "criticism" is artistic in nature, and only one of multiple aspects.

It therefore seems to me to be more sensible to proceed both with Adorno and against him, and to take as our premise a heteronomous artwork that is determined by external laws but at the same time also frames and shapes those laws autonomously, and in some cases forges an autonomous relationship with them. Effectively, this means thinking Adorno's nonrestrictive concept of autonomy through to its logical conclusion. Indeed, Adorno was constantly producing evidence of art's autonomy, while at the same time refusing to seal it off in a realm apart. In a now famous formulation, he speaks of its double character as simultaneously *fait social* and autonomous entity. To understand art as "mimetic procedure" means not only to acknowledge this double character, but also to exemplify and illustrate it. For the mimetic procedure follows a self-directed dynamic that at the same time takes its bearings from certain prior determinations. But how exactly do social constraints enter into art? For Adorno, it is the material that is charged with taking this step. It drags society with it, so to speak, and at the same time obeys its own logic. It seems to me that this approach is also useful for the analysis of contemporary artistic practices. With the decision to use a particular material—for example, printed and embroidered fabric as the substrate for an image by Cosima von Bonin—the artwork becomes heteronomous. For with the material, external constraints are imposed on the artwork. Thus, for example, the history of the recent use of fabrics (the Polke-Palermo line) involves claims and interpretations with which one has to come to terms. With the decision to create a cloth picture, the artist automatically assumes a frame of reference that cannot be shaken off, like *Schein* (that is, semblance or appearance) for Adorno. The meaning of the fabric must always be regarded as historically specific. At a particular point in time and within a particular artistic formation, the fabric is coded in a particular way. Of course, it is always entirely possible to ignore this and to turn one's back on these meanings. Contemporary practices are generally characterized by the fact that they work with these codes, signal consciousness of them, and reflect them. But not only this. They are not only heteronomous on this material level, but also as regards their economic status. They are heteronomous by dint of their commodity form, which cannot be eliminated. Artworks, in the end, are pure exchange values, and whoever produces art inevitably becomes entangled in this exchange value character of his work, that is, in the art market, with which there are naturally various ways to relate. This form of artistic heteronomy is certainly much more pronounced today than it was in the time of Adorno, for whom the art market and the culture industry were fundamentally suspect. In my view, however, the fact that cultural products are largely heteronomous does nothing to diminish their relative autonomy. Art is heteronomous and, on condition of that heteronomy, is also capable of developing autonomies. It is possible to demonstrate this especially well with the example of the mimetic procedure. Precisely the artist who proceeds mimetically commits him- or herself on the one hand to an idiosyncratic and self-directed dynamic, a dynamic that, on the other hand, is positively demanded by a prior and external determination.

Translated from the German by James Gussen

01 Theodor W.Adorno, "Those Twenties," in idem, *Critical Models: Interventions and Catchwords*, trans. Henry W. Pickford (New York: Columbia Univ. Press, 1998), 41 (hereafter cited in the text as TT).

THOSE NINETIES

Georg Schöllhammer

Slogans make themselves suspect not just because they serve to degrade thoughts into mere counters; they are also the index of their own untruth.
(Theodor W. Adorno)[01]

It is not terribly rare that the writers of the last generation of an intellectual paradigm on the wane achieve a mannered and brilliant presence in their texts. They are in a position to incorporate their former rivals into their own thinking, to permit them to affect it. They form coalitions with arguments that were once foreign to them but are now peacefully embraced by their own arguments. In this way texts emerge that are able once again to position themselves brilliantly against the foreign world of a new, raw, methodologically fresh generation whose thinking has a different basis.
In a brief meditation dedicated to the art dealer and theorist of cubism Daniel-Henry Kahnweiler, in 1963 Theodor W. Adorno reflected on the boom of a nostalgia. The short and glosslike essay is titled "Jene zwanziger Jahre," and it objects to the logic of dividing historical periods into decades that is still common today in the art industry. In this precious essay Adorno reclaimed the history of the production of aesthetic ideas from its prevalent form in the mainstream and turns it back to the raw time that, however much it may have been characterized by uncertainties and marginalizations, was permeated by a mood of artistic emergence, a time in which an aesthetic paradigm began to consolidate in what would later become the elites. And Adorno took another turn in this text, one that is almost paradigmatic for his pessimism vis-à-vis the mainstream: he characterized the popular—the approval culture with the effusive, which in a superficial reading made the 1920s nostalgia of the early 1960s, which were not exactly liberated times either, seem so gripping—as a false nostalgia. In reality, Adorno said, the fatal neglect to continue the work on the motifs from the prewar artistic emergence had already occurred in the 1920s; the precarious aspect of modernism had been exchanged for an entertainment mainstream. Behind the latter's seemingly freely conceived façades, Adorno believed, lay the work preparing the subsequent liquidation of the true potentials of the difficult and unconventional embraced by the avant-garde culture of the late turn-of-the-century period when it left behind the bourgeois consensus of late impressionist self-assurance—the very liquidation that followed from 1930 on.

Hence, 1930 was already inherent in 1920.

In 1963 Adorno was once again pointing back to the modernism of the 1910s, which he saw as the loser in this consumption based on decades; he believed it had proved a fragment that was not pursued further after the catastrophe of National Socialism and World War II because of its stylistic and formalist rigor and because it had been distorted by the mainstream of the 1920s. The project of a new aesthetics must therefore, he believed, be considered aborted and repressed, twisted and wounded, and thus would be difficult to reinstate. Consequently, even the art history of the beginning of the century could only be conceived as a series of rejections, discontinuities, ruptures, and false connections.

"Nevertheless, the idea that the twenties were a world where, as Brecht puts it in *Mahagonny*, 'everything may be permitted,' that is, a utopia, also has its truth. At that time... there seemed to be a real possibility of a politically liberated society. But it only seemed so..." (TT 43).

Theory, Etc.

In the early 1990s it was quite fashionable in the art industry of Western Europe to say that the cultural world was a political one. It was said quite generally and probably against the backdrop of the newly evolving political and cultural geographies that followed the breakdown of the socialist empire and that of the birth of another mode of production on the proscenium of the art of the 1980s, which consisted of installation painting, object, and at most video installation—that is, the birth of what came to be called New Media. Such shifts in the structure, of the sort just emerging at the time that then in fact began to inform the art industry from about 1987 onward, are often accompanied by latencies in intellectual and artistic life. This is particularly true when a material basis for the discourse sees itself as having been replaced by another discourse or when it finds itself in a crisis, as happened in the late 1980s with the art market.

At that time just such a leap that falls on latencies was occurring. A kind of reversal of Adorno's pessimistic analysis of the 1920s was taking place. Young artists associated themselves with political-conceptual art of the late 1960s and early 1970s that had been abandoned, not canonized, or not carried out; they tried to reconstruct and build on strategies from the local scene that had been concealed by the postmodern *horror conceptui* and its battles of matériel.

The repressive histories that this task saw itself confronting were sketched roughly as follows: in the early 1970s the first great cable networks of the European audiovisual media began to install that splintering of discourses on which the European, and especially French, theory of "postmodernism" would build its critical models. From the mid-1970s on, if not earlier, "postmodern" media capitalism did away with the dogmas of the sixties generation's attempt to come to terms with fascism, colonialism, capitalism, and oppression. Or media capitalism made use of these things for its own social politics, turning them into a cynical Social Darwinist neoliberalism. To give one example: Franco Basaglia and his policy of deinstitutionalizing the so-called mentally ill in the clinic in Trieste, which was a radically reformist concept that developed logically from the ideas of the emancipatory left, resulted, in the spirit of 1968, in a law that closed all the private psychiatric institutions in Italy in the 1970s. The model was admired worldwide. With his radical cuts to the budgets for health and social services in the United States during the 1980s Ronald Reagan achieved a deinstitutionalization that was nearly as total, which tossed people out of the clinics and into the streets.

For critical art from Europe and the United States during the 1970s and early 1980s, depicting the subjective against the background of this emergent mediocritization and economizing of the world—as called for by Deleuze and Guattari as well—meant displaying self-awareness, or more specifically gender and race awareness. It also meant emphasizing that socialization is by no means an arbitrary social formation but rather a process in which the ideal potential of the individual clashes with the institutions and the media as the embodiments of social conceptions. Foucault had still held out hope that an unwritten body existed, so to speak, but at the same time he made it irrefutably clear in his writings that there was no return to a model of the body—and consequently, of course, no return to a model of the subject—that is not interpreted by cultural meanings from the outset. That was the status quo.

This difference between a form of cultural production in which the producers observe themselves and attend to their own standards and criteria for success and one in which they are obliged to call upon the standards and criteria of the public—that is say, something that is always interpreted and represented elsewhere—is precisely what Adorno was pointing to in his 1963 text. He was concerned with making the distinction in order to show this exact rupture. It is the rupture between, on the one hand, culture as a way of coming to terms in the cultural realm with the control of the apparatuses of power and, on the other, the distinct number of those strategies and artifacts of an art understood as essentially new that is produced and practiced by those who are battling over other networks—networks that have their own techniques and tropes, forms and arguments.

That is why the question arises: What did we mean when we said at the end of the 1980s that art was nothing but a social construct? On what basis could we say that? There was no solid ground for criticism, and that was precisely what our criticism was supposed to express: that it was clear that there was no solid ground for criticism.

The danger came not from an excessive faith in ideological arguments, which were taken for facts; rather, it appeared in the form of an immense distrust of facts, which were misunderstood as ideological tropes.

If there are many in the art industry today—quite unlike in the early 1990s—who have these kinds of difficulties imagining categories like institutional meaning and political interpretation as the key problems of cultural analysis and who read the category of culture once again primarily against the backdrop of economic processes, then it probably has something to do with this. There is a certain historical irony in the current flirting with the centrality of theory, economy, and circulation in the analysis of culture. When a single position dominates the intellectual world it is usually not a time of creativity but a time of stagnation, a time of orthodoxy, which is only rarely still creative. That seems to me to be the case right now.

Of course, the momentum, the age of theory, is not lost, not over; the theory machines—to paraphrase a term from Deleuze—have, however, often become disproportional to their subject. No, it is something else one could say here: the word *theory* has degenerated into a codeword in the art industry for positions that are fairly easy to predict. Where the word appears, it usually appears together with ideas of social transformation, historical agency, the disposition of the self (however that is understood), the heterogeneity of cultures, a bit of Lacanian analysis of the symbolic, meager analyses of postimperial globalization, and so on. Moreover, all of this is presented in the context of a world of rancid, late Enlightenment ideas.

Military planners are frequently accused of arriving one war too late with their current planning, of not seeing the right time. It has been a while since intellectuals and artists stood at the forefront of events. Even the intellectuals in the early 1990s seemed to be arriving one confrontation too late, to have missed one battle. Just as the modernism to which the criticism of the 1960s referred had its crises in its own day, the time to react to the symptoms of crisis of the postmodernism 1980s had already passed by the early 1990s. Thus it was anything but a coincidence that the works that contained essentially the entire repertoire of possibilities of artistic expression to which the political art of the late 1980s responded had emerged in precisely the period between Berkeley 1964 (i.e., hippie culture and Black Panthers), Paris 1968 (i.e., intellectual revolt), and London 1975 (i.e., punk).
Yet another field of reference for the art of the late 1980s and its early postcolonial agenda was derived from history: during the 1960s and 1970s the interest in other "cultures" was initially defined in terms of the right of various peripheral societies to portray themselves against the empire of the West—that is, generally within the framework of the European left's romantic or ideological solidarity with the Third World. That made political sense in light of the various anticolonial struggles, of the Vietnam War, and of the crisis of the West that began in 1968. Nevertheless, "Third World" culture was always to some degree a negative ideal. Because it was problematic to define this concept—since the aesthetic canons remained, unscrutinized, those of the Western art industry—all that remained of it was a commitment to a collection of "national cultures on the path to self-determination"...
Postmodernism and its discourses on architecture and the city also broke with the high modernist discourses about poetry and music to which Adorno's text still refers with

respect to another important dichotomy of modernism—namely, the significance of the space-time relationship in the ontology of art. Poetic language and modern music, with their claim to aesthetic autonomy, which were supposed to be the examples that led the way for the other arts—for example, they inspired Clement Greenberg's paradigmatic theory of painting—rapidly disappeared as a point of reference in theoretical texts on art. The talk of time as the dominate factor of modernity and modernism and of space as that of postmodernism was significant both thematically and empirically. In his text Adorno once again evoked, without alluding to it emphatically, the field of discourse of bourgeois philosophy at the beginning of the last century—in which the older factions of neo-Kantians, idealists, evolutionists, and vitalists fought their battles against the young phenomenologists, the logical positivists, and the philosophers of language.

From today's perspective, it seems there is no longer a therapeutic possibility for working through the repressive histories of the early 1990s with a view to historical truth. It is, however, possible to point to several motives that were at work in this repression. Then the critical artists of the 1990s could perhaps be described as people being artistically active, their work could be recognized as an effect that has turned into a trace of a heterogeneous system of technological, discursive, cultural, social, and other references and practices that cannot be reduced to a narrative. And hence as something like marks of a rupture, a collapse of discontinuities both in the relations within an artistic field and in the context of a field of speaking and writing about art that seems to be almost petrified.

The difficulty in this reconstruction work is not just the executive power of the art industry vis-à-vis its participants, which both determines and distorts the archives; it is not abstractly something "false" but is the normalization and "legalization" or certain strategies of discourse and of representation itself.

The gesture of many works produced in the late 1980s and early 1990s—in the context of neoconceptual art, critical media art, and displays of political information, as well as that of works with emancipatory references to Pop Art and alternative practices but also practices related to the field of situational installations or site-specific interventions n public spaces—was itself often profoundly caught up in the modernist idea that ociety is based on discipline. At the very least it operated with a concept that space vas to be disciplined, an idea that had already become historic by adapting concepts rom the 1960s and 1970s. On the other hand, however, precisely in this historicity, his appearance of self-containedness, there is a glimmer of utopia that could be incited against the normalization strategies of the art industry: that it remains possible to levelop a distanced, even pedagogical relationship to the symbolic systems of this in-lustry that would enable one to be productive within a new, more self-determined pace. I believe that this was probably one of the main reasons—in addition to the in-luences of solidarity of a hip culture revolving around new beats and sounds—that number of very disparate parties active in scattered places throughout the continent as a networked field with shared areas of activity became increasingly self-aware and volved in opposition to the institutions of the art industry and market.

Toward the end of the decade the solidarity that resulted from institutionalized rivalry o the industry frequently broke off from a sentimental solidarity of the historical allies of a given field and from a kind of retrospective romanticizing of its circumstances. The days when people were united against a common enemy were idealized and hero-zed, as it were.

Seen from today's perspective, therefore, it may seem as questionable as it does man-nered when a group of artists explicitly evoked such moments of the historical and pre-postmodern criticism of modernism that were hardly present elsewhere in the cul-ural life of the early 1990s. Viewed against the cultural climate of these years, how-ver, it becomes clear that the point was to demonstrate codes of artistic practices that vere extracted for the purpose of dissolving the classic oppositions between the ordi-nary and the elaborated, the everyday and the sublime, and converting the opposition of politics and art into a means of production for the politics of art.

Even in the internal discussions of the proponents of such measures, however, the potentially iconoclastic energy of the field soon became evident: the project criticizing postmodernism by falling back on the criticism of modernism from the 1960s could not so easily be introduced into the canon of the 1990s because it had defined the pre-onditions of the possibilities of communication as such—as possibilities that are sublated within the disciplining spatial figures and concepts of modernism itself in the form of promises of autonomy.

"The very idea of intellectual production has been poisoned. Its self-confidence, the certainty that it is making history, is undermined. This accords with the fact that, precisely to the extent that it is assimilated, intellectual production no longer has any actual effect. Even its most extravagant expressions are no longer safe from being integrated into industrialized culture" (TT 44; translation modified).

Adorno's description here of how the cultural industriousness of the 1920s trivialized and popularized the art of the beginning of the century is similar to the way the art of the early 1990s was overwritten by its own reception, made institutionally accessible and assimilable: to reduce information and context with the goal of making the work as homogeneous as possible, to make certain that the space of activity of both the artist and the viewers was strictly controlled by an identifiable set of objects and possible movements, and to bring the motifs of the critique of modernism in parallel with a consumerist and design-oriented affirmation of the formal world of the modernism of the 1960s and 1970s in order to construct and establish a field that can be specified in terms of style but not of content.

Working in and against institutions made it necessary to accept this contradiction in exchange for the institutionalization of intentions that reproduces the power of these institutions. By contrast, becoming institutionalized means satisfying the needs of the institutions in their search for new, more discrete or more direct ways to extend their position. I believe this was one of the major contradictions of the first half of the 1990s: the conflict between the call for criticism, on the one hand, and the awareness of the specialized task and role of the individual artist within the structure of the industry that the critique was addressing, on the other, was not sufficiently thought through in terms of the status of authorship and autonomy.

In a figure like Adorno's—with its elitist insistence on the position of authorship, on an essential, inalienable relic of subjectivity, of identity; with its profoundly conflicting persistence on the residues of an idealistic, bourgeois role for the artist, which can also be seen as a naïve liberal-humanist universalism—and in this codification of a remnant, one also finds preserved a potential for resistance against a social reality of the institutional structures of power that seek to incapacitate that remnant.

With respect to the artistic emergence of the early 1990s, too, one could remark with Adorno: "The tradition, including the tradition of anti-traditionalism, was broken off, and half-forgotten tasks remain. (...) The impulses must be recovered that in the vaunted twenties were already threatening to petrify or dissipate" (TT 45–46). In the case of the 1990s, at least, the success of an art history based on epochs does not rest solely on the fact that it often depicts hegemonic relationships as the cultural climate of the period, or as its nature in the history of style and ideas. Its success is also based on whether it succeeds—while suppressing the political nature of the symbolic itself—in causing the epoch's "form of expression," revised with an eye to its trademark-like core, to reverberate.

In his critique of the 1920s Adorno was not simply concerned with biographical sentimentality and defending the empire of his own value judgments against appropriation by what he usually referred to as the culture industry. He was concerned about more than that: namely, about the questions always inherent in his writings on music, for example: what is the specific space that the representations of art can produce? What can be said unequivocally given the contradictions of the aesthetic and of its analysis as a means of production? That are important questions for the art of those nineties as well, although it has largely gone unanswered.

Translated from the German by Steven Lindberg

THE AUTHORS

Isabelle Graw

Studied Political Science in Paris, works as an art critic and lives in Berlin. She published many texts in art magazines and is professor for Art Theory at Städelschule in Frankfurt am Main. Publications include *Silberblick. Texte zu Kunst und Politik* (Berlin 1999), *Die bessere Hälfte. Künstlerinnen im 20. und 21. Jahrhhundert* (Cologne 2003).

Georg Schöllhammer

Is editor of *springerin – Hefte zur Gegenwartskunst.*

PHOTOCREDITS / LIST OF WORKS

Christopher Williams

* Model: 1964 Renault Dauphine-Four, R-1095. Body Type & Seating: 4-dr-sedan- 4 to 5 persons
Engine Type: 14/52 Weight: 1397 lbs
Price: $ 1495,00 USD (original)
ENGINE DATA: Base four: inline, overhead-valve four-cylinder. Cast iron block and aluminum head. W/removable cylinder sleeves. Displacement: 51.5 cu.in (845 oc.) Bore and stroke: 2.28x3.15 in.
(58 x 80 mm) Compression Ratio: 7.25:1 Brake Horsepower: 32 (SAE) at 4200 rpm
Torque: 50 lbs. At 2000 rpm, Three main bearings. Solid valve lifters. Single downdraft carburetor.
CHASSIS DATA: Wheelbase: 89 in. Overall length: 155 in. Height: 57 in. Width: 60 in. Front thread: 49 in. Rear thread: 48 in. Standard Tires: 5.50 x 15
TECHNICAL: Layout: rear engine, rear drive. Transmission: four speed manual. Stearing: rack and pinion. Suspension (front): independent coil springs. Brakes: front/rear disc. Body construction: steel unibody.
PRODUCTION DATA: Sales: 18,432 sold in U.S. in 1964 (all types). Manufacturer: Regie Nationale des Usines Renault, Billancourt, France. Distributor: Renault Inc., New York, NY, U.S.A.
Serial number: R-10950059799
Engine number: Type 670-05 # 191 563
California License Plate number: UOU 087
Vehicle ID Number: 0059799
January 15, 2000
2000 (No. 6)
Gelatin silver print
64,5 x 74,5 cm
Edition of 10
Wilhelm and Gaby Schürmann

Markus Schinwald

* Adornorama, 2003
25 x 25 x 25 cm
Courtesy Georg Kargl, Vienna

John Massey

* As the Hammer Strikes (A Partial Illustration), 1982
3-channel synchronized DVD installation, 30 minutes
(Reconstruction of the 16mm film installation)
National Gallery of Canada, Ottawa

Bruce Nauman

* Concrete Tape Recorder Piece, 1968
Concrete, tape recorder, tape roll
30,5 x 61 x 61 cm
Flick Collection
Photo: A. Burger, Zurich

Louise Lawler

* Untitled (Collection of 60 Drawings), 1993
Cibachrome, felt, crystal
Hight: 5,08 cm, ø: 8,89 cm
Courtesy Monika Sprüth Philomene Magers, Cologne

* Untitled (Attachments), 1993
Cibachrome, felt, crystal
Hight: 5,08 cm, ø: 8,89 cm
Courtesy Monika Sprüth Philomene Magers, Cologne

Lawrence Weiner

* MISCELLANOUS OBJECTS (MADE BY HAND) GIVEN TO THE TIDE FOR A TIME, 1989
Writing on wall
Sammlung Osarek, Potsdam

Gustav Metzger

* Modell eines auto-destruktiven Monuments, 1960
(reconstruction 1997)
33 x 14,5 x 12 cm
Estate of the artist

*Auto-destructive Art, 1959/60
Manifesto
Estate of the artist
(without illustration)

Kirsten Pieroth

* Postkarten aus Berlin, 2002
45 postcards, 45 computer prints
10 x 14,8 cm each
Courtesy Klosterfelde, Berlin
(without illustration)

Brief nach Berlin, 2003
Brief nach Berlin, der am 29. April 2003 in einen deutschen Breifkasten im Postmuseum in Kairo eingeworfen wurde.
Courtesy Klosterfelde, Berlin (illustration)

Mein Flug über den Ozean, 2002
Lindberg book, stamps, cord
4,5 x 20,8 x 14 cm
Courtesy De Chiara Gallery, New York
(illustration)

Euan Macdonald

* Poor Blumfeld, 2002
2 DVDs, 2 monitors
Courtesy Cohan and Leslie, New York and Zink & Gegner, Munich

Christopher Williams

* Model: 1964 Renault Dauphine-Four, R-1095. Body Type & Seating: 4-dr-sedan- 4 to 5 persons
Engine Type: 14/52 Weight: 1397 lbs
Price: $ 1495,00 USD (original)
ENGINE DATA: Base four: inline, overhead-valve four-cylinder. Cast iron block and aluminum head. W/removable cylinder sleeves. Displacement: 51.5 cu.in (845 oc.) Bore and stroke: 2.28x3.15 in. (58 x 80 mm) Compression Ratio: 7.25:1 Brake Horsepower: 32 (SAE) at 4200 rpm
Torque: 50 lbs. At 2000 rpm, Three main bearings. Solid valve lifters. Single downdraft carburetor.
CHASSIS DATA: Wheelbase: 89 in. Overall length: 155 in. Height: 57 in. Width: 60 in. Front thread: 49 in. Rear thread: 48 in. Standard Tires: 5.50 x 15
TECHNICAL: Layout: rear engine, rear drive. Transmission: four speed manual. Stearing: rack and pinion. Suspension (front): independent coil springs. Brakes: front/rear disc. Body construction: steel unibody.
PRODUCTION DATA: Sales: 18,432 sold in U.S. in 1964 (all types).
Manufacturer: Regie Nationale des Usines Renault, Billancourt, France.
Distributor: Renault Inc., New York, NY, U.S.A.
Serial number: R-10950059799
Engine number: Type 670-05 # 191 563
California License Plate number: UOU 087
Vehicle ID Number: 0059799
January 15, 2000
2000 (No. 10)
Gelatin silver print
64,5 x 74,5 cm
Edition of 10
Wilhelm and Gaby Schürmann

Henrik Plenge Jakobsen

* Kapital Melankolie (Prismatisch), 2003
Circular sawblades, prism, bolts
35 x 35 x 6 cm
Courtesy Galleri Nicolai Wallner, Copenhagen

* Kapital Melankolie (Chromatisch), 2003
Vinyl record, fluorite, bolts
30 x 30 x 5 cm
Courtesy Galleri Nicolai Wallner, Copenhagen

* Kapital Melankolie (Zwölfton), 2003
Record player, circular sawblade, fluorite
10 x 33 x 44 cm
Courtesy Galleri Nicolai Wallner, Copenhagen

Cerith Wyn Evans

* Adorno Centenary ("The Stars Down to Earth" published 1974), 2003
Artemide lamp (Miconos Sospensione), flat screen monitor, Morse code unit, computer
Dimensions Variable
Courtesy Galerie Daniel Buchholz, Cologne
(without illustration)

Cleave 02 (The Accursed Share), 2002
Mirror ball, lamp, blinds, laptop computer, shutter, plants, text by George Bataille
Dimensions variable
Courtesy White Cube, London
(illustration)

Liam Gillick

* Discussion Island Reconciliation Plates, 1997
4 sheets of aluminium, screws, doomed covers for screws
100 x 200 cm
Courtesy Schipper & Krome, Berlin
(without illustration)

(The What If? Scenario) Mirrored Insulation Plate, 1996
Sheet of aluminium, screws, doomed covers for screws
100 x 200 cm
Courtesy Schipper & Krome, Berlin
(illustration)

Martin Creed

* The lights going on and off
Work No. 127, 1995
Dimensions variable
Courtesy Johnen + Schöttle, Cologne
(without illustration)

Work No. 270
The lights off, 2001
Installation view Johnen + Schöttle, Cologne
(illustration)

Maria Eichhorn

* 6 Kästen Mineralwasser (SPA) /
7 Gläser, 1995
Sammlung Anja Lohmüller
Courtesy Galerie Barbara Weiss
Photo: Jens Ziehe

Jason Dodge

* Why are you afraid of distances, 2003
Aluminium, cable, Dimensions variable
Courtesy Casey Kaplan, New York

Martin Boyce

* Untitled (After Rietveld), 1999
Neon lights, steel band
183 x 183 x 183 cm
Sammlung Haubrok
Photo © Martin Boyce and The Modern Institute, Glasgow

Andreas Slominski

* Untitled, 1987
Fabric, 10 x 20 x 19 cm
Museum für Moderne Kunst,
Frankfurt am Main
Permanent loan to the Museum für Moderne Kunst, Frankfurt am Main
Photo: Rudolf Nagel

* Untitled, 1990
Cardboard, paper, cloth
78,3 x 55,4 cm
Museum für Moderne Kunst,
Frankfurt am Main
Photo: Rudolf Nagel

Ad Reinhardt

* Bild Nr. 16, 1955
Oil on canvas, 203,5 x 101,5 cm
Museum Wiesbaden,
Permanent loan of Museumsverein Otto Ritschl e.V.
Photo: Ed Restle

Jonathan Monk

* High School Boogie-Woogie, 2002
16mm film, loop, Cube size: 5,7 cm
Collection of Nell and Jack Wendler,
London
Courtesy Casey Kaplan, New York
Photo: Dave Morgan

* Sol LeWitt's Twenty First Sentence on Conceptual Art: From One Restaurant To The Next (Frankfurt am Main), 2003
24 pieces, paper
Courtesy Meyer Riegger Galerie, Karlsruhe
(without illustration)

Gerhard Richter

* Grau, 1976
Oil on canvas
200 x 200 cm
Private collection
Photo: Rudolf Nagel

Mathias Poledna

* Western Recording, 2003
16mm film
10:30 min
Courtesy Richard Telles Fine Art, Los Angeles and Galerie Meyer Kainer, Vienna

Stephen Prina

An Evening of 19th and 20th Century Piano Music, LACE, Los Angeles 1986
(Poster)

An Evening of 19th and 20th Century Piano Music, Museum of Contemporary Art, Los Angeles 1988
(Programme guide)

An Evening of 19th and 20th Century Piano Music. Museum of Contemporary Art, Los Angeles, 1988
(Invitation)
Courtesy Gisela Capitain, Cologne

Christopher Williams

* Model: 1964 Renault Dauphine-Four, R-1095. Body Type & Seating: 4-dr-sedan- 4 to 5 persons
Engine Type: 14/52 Weight: 1397 lbs
Price: $ 1495,00 USD (original)
ENGINE DATA: Base four: inline, overhead-valve four-cylinder. Cast iron block and aluminum head.
W/removable cylinder sleeves. Displacement: 51.5 cu.in (845 oc.) Bore and stroke: 2.28x3.15 in.
(58 x 80 mm) Compression Ratio: 7.25:1 Brake Horsepower: 32 (SAE) at 4200 rpm
Torque: 50 lbs. At 2000 rpm, Three main bearings. Solid valve lifters.
Single downdraft carburetor.
CHASSIS DATA: Wheelbase: 89 in. Overall length: 155 in. Height: 57 in. Width: 60 in. Front thread: 49 in. Rear thread: 48 in. Standard Tires: 5.50 x 15
TECHNICAL: Layout: rear engine, rear drive. Transmission: four speed manual. Stearing: rack and pinion. Suspension (front): independent coil springs.
Brakes: front/rear disc. Body construction: steel unibody.
PRODUCTION DATA: Sales: 18,432 sold in U.S. in 1964 (all types).
Manufacturer: Regie Nationale des Usine

Renault, Billancourt, France.
Distributor: Renault Inc., New York,
NY, U.S.A.
Serial number: R-10950059799
Engine number: Type 670-05 # 191 563
California License Plate number: UOU 087
Vehicle ID Number: 0059799
anuary 15, 2000
2000 (No. 9)
Gelatin silver print
4,5 x 74,5 cm
Edition of 10
Wilhelm and Gaby Schürmann

Peter Friedl
Untitled (badly organized), 2003
Glass letters, neon
70 x 260 x 6 cm

Samuel Beckett
Quad I & II (Quadrat I & II)
roduced 1981, premier broadcast 1982
Quad I: 15 min
Quad II: 5 min
Courtesy Éditions De Minuit, Paris
© Südwestfunk Stuttgart

Carl Andre
* Aluminium-Steel Dipole (E/W), 1973
2 pieces, side to side
Aluminium east, steel west
0,5 x 100 x 100 cm
Sammlung Osarek, Berlin

Thomas Demand
* Simulator, 2003
C-print/diasec, 465 x 330 cm
Courtesy Schipper & Krome, Berlin
(illustration: draft of the work)

Andre Cadere
* Barre de bois ronde
Painted wood, 198 x 2 cm
Collection FRAC Nord – Pas de Calais
Dunkerque
Photo: E. Watteau

Art & Language
* Untitled Painting, 1965
Mirror mounted on canvas
2 pieces, 119,3 x 58,3 x 10,9 cm each
Courtesy Lisson Gallery, London
Photo: Stephen White, London

Secret Painting, 1967-68
Acrylic on canvas and photostat
2 pieces, 97 x 97 cm each
Courtesy Lisson Gallery, London
Photo: Gareth Winters
(not shown in the exhibition)

Sarah Morris

* Library of Congress [Capital], 2001
Household gloss on canvas,
214 x 214 x 5 cm
Sammlung Goetz
Photo: courtesy Sammlung Goetz
Stephen White

* Worldbank [Capital], 2001
Household gloss on canvas,
152,5 x 152,5 cm
Collection Goetz
Photo: courtesy White Cube, London
Stephen White

Isa Genzken

* Untitled (Weltempfänger)
Concrete, metal
30 x 43,3 x 8,5 cm
Courtesy Galerie Daniel Buchholz,
Cologne (without illustration)

* "Rudolf" (Weltempfänger), 1990
Concrete, metal
72 x 44,5 x 9,5 cm
Courtesy Galerie Daniel Buchholz,
Cologne (without illustration)

* Untitled (Weltempfänger), 1999
Concrete, metal
36 x 24 x 7,6 cm
Courtesy Galerie Daniel Buchholz,
Cologne (without illustration)

Weltempfänger, 1988-89
Concrete, metal
Dimensions variable
Installation view
Courtesy Galerie Daniel Buchholz,
Cologne (illustration)

Weltempfänger, 1992
Concrete, metal
10 x 30 x 5 cm
Courtesy Galerie Daniel Buchholz,
Cologne (illustration)

Florian Pumhösl

* Village, Museum, 2002
University of Dar Es Salaam, Library
C-Print on DIFO, 45 x 30 cm
Courtesy Galerie Krobath Wimmer,
Vienna

* Village, Museum, 2002
University of Dar Es Salaam, Housing
Units
C-Print on DIFO, 45 x 30 cm
Courtesy Galerie Krobath Wimmer,
Vienna
without illustration)

* Village, Museum, 2002
Ceramics Factory, Dodoma
C-Print on DIFO, 45 x 30 cm
Courtesy Galerie Krobath Wimmer,
Vienna
without illustration)

works shown in the exhibition

ACKNOWLEDGEMENTS

Daniel Buchholz, Cologne
Gisela Capitain, Cologne
Collection FRAC Nord - Pas de Calais, Dunkerque
Flick Collection
Sammlung Goetz
Sammlung Haubrok, Düsseldorf
Johnen + Schöttle, Cologne
Georg Kargel, Vienna
Klosterfelde, Berlin
Krobath Wimmer, Vienna
Lisson Gallery, London
Sammlung Anja Lohmüller, Berlin
Meyer Kainer, Vienna
Museum für Moderne Kunst, Frankfurt am Main
Museum Wiesbaden
National Gallery of Canada, Ottawa
Sammlung Osarek, Berlin
Schipper & Krome, Berlin
Wilhelm und Gaby Schürmann, Aachen
Monika Sprüth Philomene Magers, Cologne
Galleri Nicolai Wallner, Copenhagen
White Cube, London
Zink & Gegner, Munich
and private lenders who wish not to be mentioned.

CARL ANDRE

ART & LANGUAGE

SAMUEL BECKETT

MARTIN BOYCE

ANDRE CADERE

MARTIN CREED

THOMAS DEMAND

JASON DODGE

MARIA EICHHORN

PETER FRIEDL

ISA GENZKEN

LIAM GILLICK

HENRIK PLENGE JAKOBSEN

LOUISE LAWLER

EUAN MACDONALD

JOHN MASSEY

GUSTAV METZGER
JONATHAN MONK
SARAH MORRIS
BRUCE NAUMAN
KIRSTEN PIEROTH
MATHIAS POLEDNA
STEPHEN PRINA
FLORIAN PUMHÖSL
AD REINHARDT
GERHARD RICHTER
MARKUS SCHINWALD
ANDREAS SLOMINSKI
LAWRENCE WEINER
CHRISTOPHER WILLIAMS
CERITH WYN EVANS

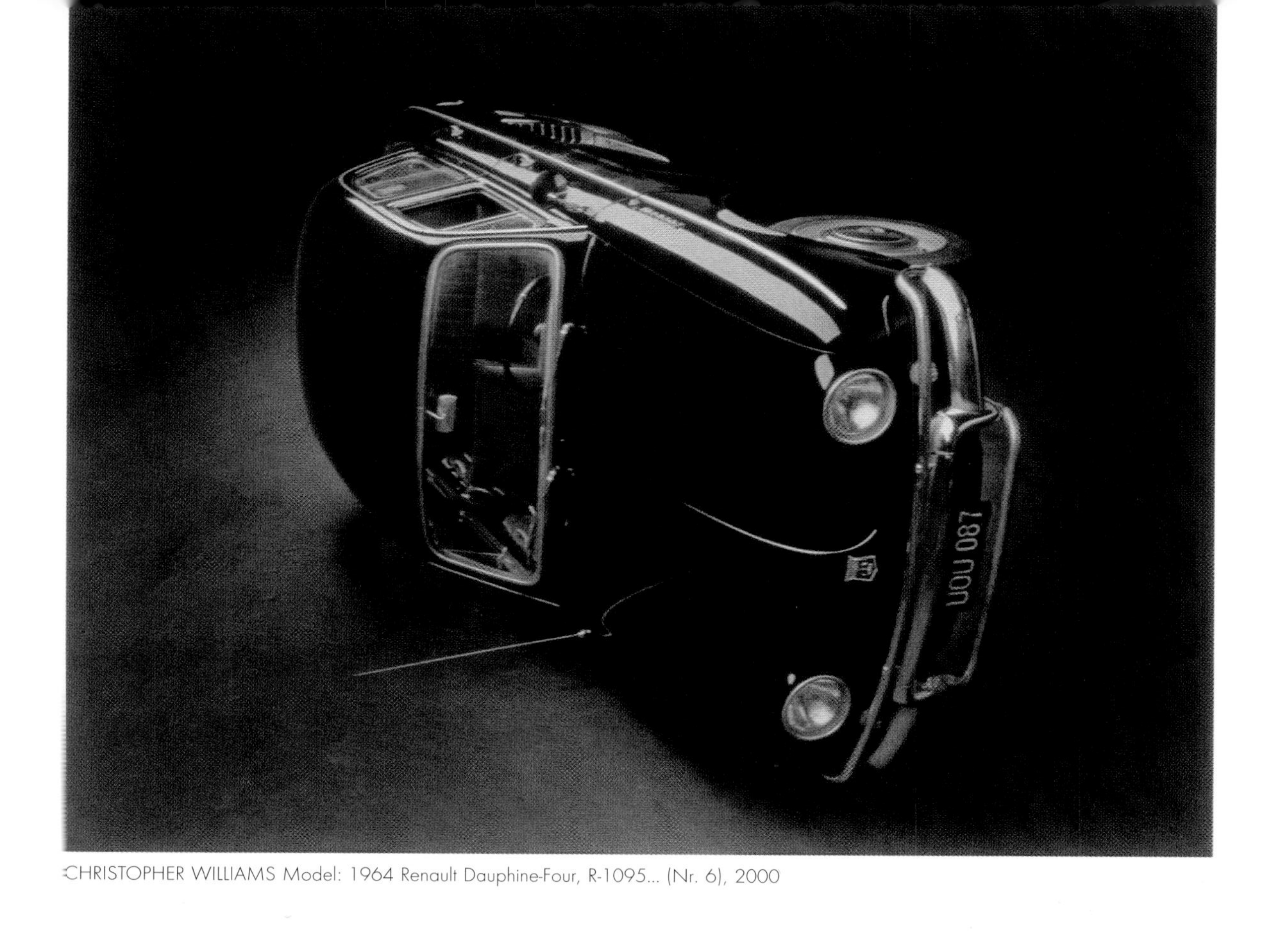

CHRISTOPHER WILLIAMS Model: 1964 Renault Dauphine-Four, R-1095... (Nr. 6), 2000

MARKUS SCHINWALD *Adornorama*, 2003

JOHN MASSEY As the Hammer Strikes (A Partial Illustration), 1982

BRUCE NAUMAN Concrete Tape Recorder Piece, 1968

LOUISE LAWLER Untitled (Collection of 60 Drawings), 1993

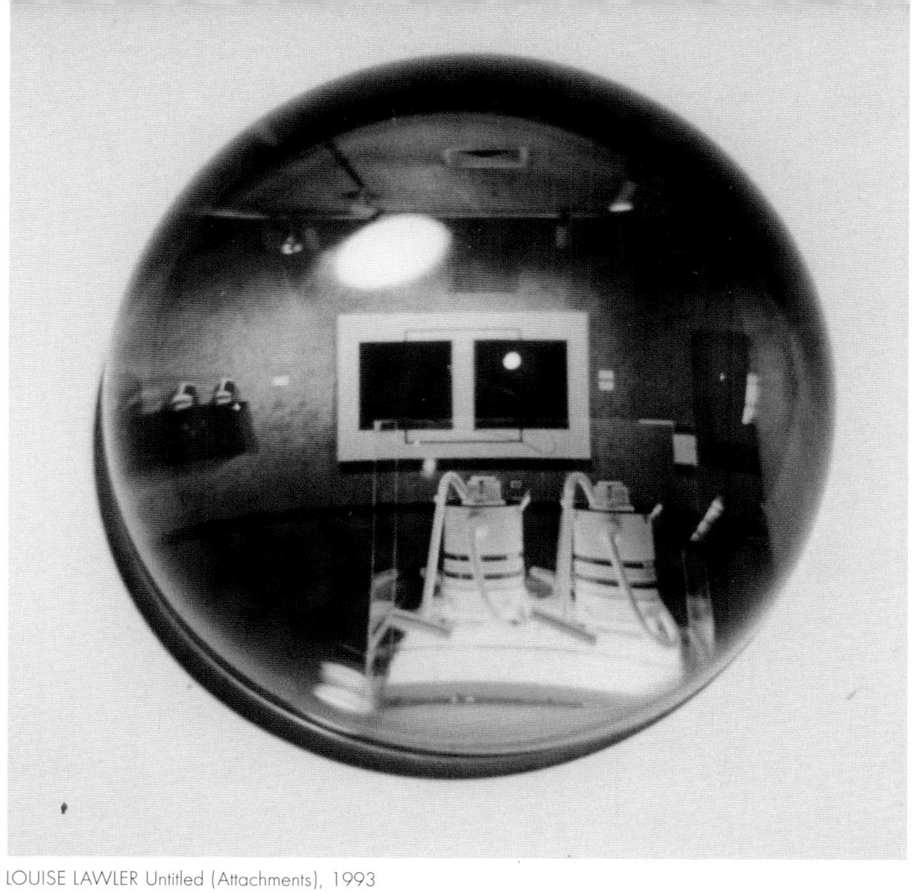

LOUISE LAWLER Untitled (Attachments), 1993

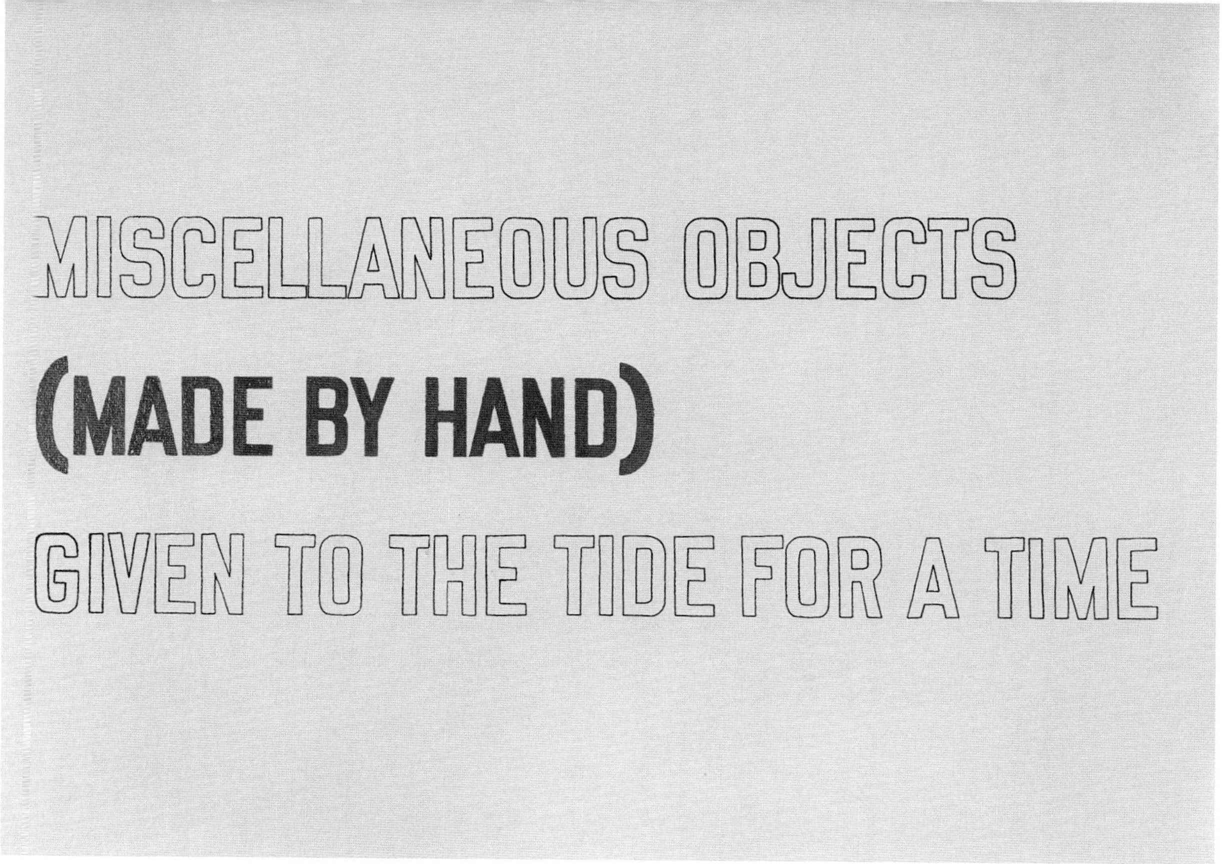

MISCELLANEOUS OBJECTS
(MADE BY HAND)
GIVEN TO THE TIDE FOR A TIME

LAWRENCE WEINER MISCELLANEOUS OBJECTS (MADE BY HAND) GIVEN TO THE TIDE FOR A TIME, 1989

GUSTAV METZGER Modell eines auto-destruktiven Monuments, 1960 (Rekonstruktion 1997)

KIRSTEN PIEROTH Brief nach Berlin, 2003

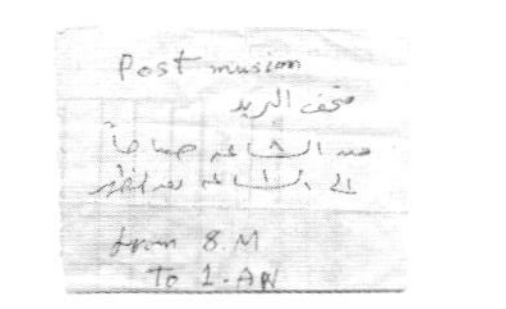

Brief nach Berlin, der am 29. April 2003
in einen deutschen Briefkasten
im Postmuseum Kairo eingeworfen wurde.

خطاب إلى برلين، مرسل فى يوم ٢٩ ابريل ٢٠٠٢
من صندوق بريد ألماني موجود بمتحف البريد فى القاهرة

KIRSTEN PIEROTH Mein Flug über den Ozean, 2002

Herausgeber: Nicolaus Schafhausen, Vanessa Joan Müller und Michael Hirsch
Gestaltung: Miriam Rech, Markus Weisbeck,
Surface Gesellschaft für Gestaltung, Frankfurt am Main
Druck und Bindung: Druckerei Lembeck, Frankfurt am Main
Logo Design: Richard Massey und Sarah Morris

Diese Publikation erscheint anläßlich der Ausstellung „adorno"
im Frankfurter Kunstverein, 29. Oktober 2003 – 4. Januar 2004

ISBN 0-9726806-3-2
ISBN 0-9726806-4-0 (Textband)
ISBN 0-9726806-5-9 (2-bändige Ausgabe)

Lukas & Sternberg
Caroline Schneider
1182 Broadway #1602
New York NY 10001
Linienstraße 159
D-10115 Berlin
mail@lukas-sternberg.com
www.lukas-sternberg.com

gefördert durch die

kulturstiftung des bundes

hessische kultur stiftung

Diese Publikation wird zusätzlich gefördert durch die Stadt Frankfurt am Main
und die Georg und Franziska Speyer'sche Hochschulstiftung.

frankfurterkunstverein

Steinernes Haus am Römerberg, Markt 44, D-60311 Frankfurt am Main, www.fkv.de

ADORNO

DIE MÖGLICHKEIT DES UNMÖGLICHEN

LUKAS & STERNBERG

01 Theodor W. Adorno, *Ästhetische Theorie*, Frankfurt am Main 1989, S. 337.
02 Ebd., S. 55.

VORWORT

Kunst, das ist für Adorno vor allem Musik, dann Literatur, dann Malerei. Oft ist in seinen Schriften unspezifisch vom „Kunstwerk“ die Rede. Konkrete Werke der bildenden Kunst hingegen spielen eine eher untergeordnete Rolle im Werk des Autors der *Ästhetischen Theorie*. Es geht Adorno allerdings auch weniger um die Analyse existierender künstlerischer Produktion als um das Potential, das der Kunst innerhalb des gesellschaftlichen Systems innewohnt. Kunst ist jener ästhetische Raum von Utopie, die an anderer Stelle noch nicht realisiert ist – sie steht stellvertretend für das Andere, für das aus den Produktions- und Reproduktionsprozessen Ausgenommene. Die für das Denken Adornos zentrale Hoffnung, zumindest in der Kunst könne sich eine Alternative zu den bestehenden Verhältnissen andeuten, lässt diese zur produktiven Leerstelle werden. Denn sie ist allem voran ein Hinweis darauf, daß es dieses „Andere“, dieses Außerhalb der real existierenden Gesellschaft, der „verwalteten Welt“ überhaupt geben könnte, ohne daß damit die Utopie bereits eingelöst wäre. „Kunstwerke sind die Statthalter der nicht länger vom Tausch verunstalteten Dinge“,[01] heißt es in der *Ästhetischen Theorie*, und an anderer Stelle: „Zentral unter den gegenwärtigen Antinomien ist, daß Kunst Utopie sein muß und will und zwar desto entschiedener, je mehr der reale Funktionszusammenhang Utopie verbaut; daß sie aber, um nicht Utopie an Schein und Trost zu verraten, nicht Utopie sein darf.“[02]
Allein die Kunst besitzt scheinbar das Vermögen, Erfahrungen des „Außerhalb“ zu ermöglichen und, mehr noch, zur Sprache zu bringen. Für Adorno bildet die als autonome verstandene Kunst einen Gegenpart zu der alles beherrschenden Kulturindustrie und ihrer Verdoppelung der Wirklichkeit, die über den wirklichen Zustand der Welt nur hinwegtäuscht. Das setzt allerdings voraus, das Kunstwerk aus allen Kontexten dieser Kulturindustrie und ihrer Verwertungsmechanismen herauszulösen. Kunst muß ein Abstraktum bleiben, ein allen, sei es kommerziellen oder institutionellen Zurichtungen enthobenes Artefakt. In letzter Konsequenz muß sie selbst ihren Status als Kunst aufgeben und übergehen in Erkenntnis.

Adornos Vokabular ist ein radikal modernes, das sich, aus der Perspektive künstlerischer Produktion betrachtet, mit jener Nachkriegsavantgarde verbindet, deren Zeitgenosse er war. Das Aufkommen der Abstraktion, ja die Rhetorik der Avantgarde an sich, der

03 Theodor W. Adorno, *Minima Moralia*, Gesammelte Werke 4, S. 83.

es stets um die Überwindung des Bestehenden, der Suche nach dem Absoluten geht, bilden zentrale Motive der *Ästhetischen Theorie*. Das Nicht-Figurative dieser Kunst, die sich eindeutigen Aussagen verweigert, manifestiert sich für Adorno in der Formwerdung des ästhetischen Materials übereinstimmend mit dem objektiven geschichtlichen Stand der externen, nicht-künstlerischen Wirklichkeit. Allein die sich dieser Wirklichkeit radikal entziehende oder die realen Verhältnisse kritisch überbietende Kunst schafft ein Bewußtsein von der realen Negativität der Welt.
Auch deshalb steht das Kunstwerk für sich – herausgelöst aus den ökonomischen Zusammenhängen, denen es aller Autonomie zum Trotz letztlich immer unterliegt, und auch unabhängig von dem institutionellen Rahmen, in den es eingebunden ist. Nur an wenigen Stellen hat Adorno diesen Rahmen berücksichtigt, dessen Kunst bedarf, um ihre Wirkung entfalten zu können. Kunst*ausstellungen* haben ihn kaum interessiert, denn das Nebeneinander verschiedener Werke verträgt sich nicht mit dem Gedanken, jedes Werk besitze einen impliziten Alleinvertretungsanspruch für die ganze Gattung. Für Adorno zielt jedes Werk auf das Absolute und strebt damit nach der Überwindung der Kunst an sich – er spricht in der *Minima Moralia* sogar vom „Selbstvernichtungsdrang der Kunstwerke" [03] als ihrem innersten Anliegen.
Die utopische Funktion der Kunst ist ihre Funktionslosigkeit – genau in diesem Punkt liegt vielleicht der radikale Dissens zu großen Teilen der zeitgenössischen künstlerischen Praxis, denn gerade die Kunst – nimmt man Ausstellungen wie die letzte *Documenta* als Seismograph aktueller Tendenzen – scheint zum Terrain geworden zu sein, auf dem sich Defizite oder auch Ungerechtigkeiten des Politischen, Gesellschaftlichen sichtbar machen lassen. Kunst versteht sich zunehmend als Instrument der Sichtbarmachung, bezogen auf das Jetzt und die konkreten Zusammenhänge, aus denen heraus Gesellschaft sich formiert. Das macht Adornos Theorie der Kunst heute problematisch, denn auch die Überbietungsrhetorik der Avantgarde ist selbst zu einer klassischen Formel geworden. Kunst ist auf allen Ebenen institutionalisiert und fester Teil des gesellschaftlichen Systems mit seinen immer offener formulierten ökonomischen Verwertungszusammenhängen geworden. Der Glaube an die utopische Kraft der Kunst, jene radikal andere, gleichwohl nur einen winzigen Schritt vom Bestehenden entfernte Welt anzudeuten, scheint verloren.

Man könnte weiten Feldern der Gegenwartskunst vorwerfen, sich der Sehnsucht nach einer umstandslosen Identifikation avancierter politischer/gesellschaftlicher und künstlerischer/ästhetischer Anliegen hinzugeben. Gerade der zeitgenössische Kunstbetrieb nimmt in großen Teilen eine Verschiebung von jenem von Adorno noch für zentral gehaltenen Rätselcharakter von Kunstwerken hin zu Kunstwerken als Trägern einer diskursiven Bedeutung, Aussage oder Position vor. Ein solcher Pragmatismus steht Adornos Denken radikal fern. Gerade das Sich-Einlassen auf die Gesellschaft affirmiert letztlich ihre Bedingungen, könnte man mit Adorno argumentieren. Andererseits bedeutet eine Hinwendung zu politischen oder gesellschaftlichen Anliegen aber auch keine bedingungslose Aufkündigung des immanenten Rätselcharakters der Kunst. Das von Benjamin forcierte Programm einer Auslösung von Kunst in Leben oder Kunst in Politik scheint zwar vordergründig noch immer aktuell, tatsächlich ist es jedoch gerade der Kunstcharakter der Kunst, der ihr als dem noch immer vom Alltäglichen unaufhebbar Verschiedenen ihr wirkungsmächtiges Potential verleiht.

Die Ausstellungen des Frankfurter Kunstvereins, die sich in vergangenen Projekten mit programmatischen Titeln wie *Neue Welt*, *non-places* oder *nation* spiegelt, hätten Adorno bestimmt nicht gefallen. Daß gerade diese Institution im Jahr seines 100. Geburtstages eine Ausstellung unter das Motto „adorno“ stellt, mag deshalb verwundern. Gleichwohl geht es uns nicht darum, Adornos Gedanken zur Kunst in ausgewählten Kunstwerken gleichsam zu bebildern, denn weder die thesenartige Verkürzung noch die illustrative Veranschaulichung würde der Komplexität und Radikalität seiner Instrumentierung der Kunst als letztem verbliebenen Hoffnungsträger einer vor allem in ihrer Negativität beschreibbaren Gesellschaft gerecht.
Die Ausstellung im Frankfurter Kunstverein versammelt denn auch Werke der zeitgenössischen Kunst – Kunstwerke also, die in einer Zeit entstanden sind, in der sich die bildende Kunst selbst stark gegenüber jenen Positionen der avancierten Nachkriegskunst verändert hat.
Werke von Ad Reinhardt, Gustav Metzger, Bruce Nauman und Gerhard Richter bilden, chronologisch betrachtet, den Anfangspunkt der Ausstellung, speziell für das Projekt entwickelte, zum Teil direkt auf Texte Adornos sich beziehende Arbeiten

von Peter Friedl, Henrik Plenge Jakobsen, Markus Schinwald und Cerith Wyn Evans den Endpunkt. Viele Werke erhalten ihren Bezug zum Denken Adornos erst im Kontext der Ausstellung. Es geht insofern eher um eine Annäherung an sein Denken denn um eine Beweisführung, die dessen Aktualität zur Schau stellen will.

Während der erste Band dieser Publikation Essays verschiedener Philosophen und Kulturwissenschaftler versammelt, die das Denken Adornos auf seine Aktualität hin befragen und gleichermaßen seine großen gesellschaftstheoretischen Entwürfe und die Mikroebenen seiner Schriften ins Zentrum stellen, geht es in diesem Band, der auch die in der Ausstellung vertretenen Werke vorstellt, vor allem um das Verhältnis Adornos zur Bildenden Kunst.

Wir möchten an dieser Stelle vor allem der Kulturstiftung des Bundes für die Unterstützung der Ausstellung und der zweiteiligen Publikation danken. Ebenfalls gilt unser Dank der Stadt Frankfurt am Main für ihre Unterstützung. Wir danken der Hessischen Kulturstiftung und der Georg und Franziska Speyer'sche Hochschulstiftung, die die Publikation gefördert haben, sowie der Art Frankfurt für die zusätzliche Förderung der Ausstellung. Vor allem aber gilt unser Dank den Autoren und nicht zuletzt den Künstlerinnen und Künstlern, die mit ihren Werken und Ideen diese Ausstellung überhaupt erst möglich gemacht haben.

Vanessa Joan Müller, Nicolaus Schafhausen
September 2003

[01] Vgl. Theodor W. Adorno, Der wunderliche Realist. Über Siegfried Kracauer, in: Rolf Tiedemann (Hg.) unter Mitwirkung von Gretel Adorno, Susan Buck-Morss und Klaus Schultz, *Gesammelte Schriften 11. Noten zur Literatur*, Frankfurt am Main 1974, S. 388-408, hier S. 391.

[02] Vgl. André Breton, Erstes Manifest des Surrealismus, 1924, in: Ders.: *Die Manifeste des Surrealismus*, Reinbek bei Hamburg 1986, S. 11- 43.

[03] Vgl. Theodor W. Adorno, *Ästhetische Theorie* (hrsg. von Gretel Adorno u. Rolf Tiedemann), Frankfurt am Main 1989, S. 86.

ADORNO IST UNTER UNS

abelle Graw

. Mit verbundenen Augen

enken mit dem Bleistift in der Hand – mit diesem Bild hat Adorno die Arbeitsweise
eines Mentors und Freundes Siegfried Kracauer umschrieben.[01] Eine Formulierung,
ie nebenbei bemerkt an André Bretons Charakterisierung der *écriture automatique* als
ine dem „Denkstrom“ unmittelbar folgende Schreibtechnik erinnert.[02] Dieses Bild
ar als Kompliment gemeint – eine der zahlreichen Metaphern Adornos für ein mime-
sches *Verhalten*, das ihn interessierte, wenn es ihn nicht sogar faszinierte. Denkt
racauer Adorno zufolge mit dem Bleistift in der Hand, dann bedeutet dies, daß bei
m das Denken gleichsam unmittelbar in den Bleistift fließt und umgekehrt von
essen Bewegung mitgezogen wird. Mimetisch ist dieses Denken insofern, als es die
ewegungen, die die Hand mit dem Bleistift tätigt, nachvollzieht. Dieses Mimesis-
erständnis, das nicht Abbildung der Wirklichkeit, sondern eine Konservierung des
imetischen Vermögens im künstlerischen Prozeß behauptet, ist einer der wichtig-
en Topoi des Modernismus, ein Topos, der sich auch durch die bildende Kunst des
0. Jahrhunderts zieht und häufig in ihr thematisch wurde. Man denke nur an Paul
lees berühmten Ausspruch, daß das Auge dem Weg folge, der ihm vom Werk vorge-
eichnet würde – eine Art modernistisches Credo, mit dem er sich zum bloß Ausfüh-
enden einer höheren Ordnung stilisierte. Dieses Motto trägt aber auch *einem* wesent-
chen Aspekt künstlerischer Produktion Rechnung: dem mimetischen Impuls. Die
erie der *Blind Drawings* von Robert Morris aus den siebziger Jahren könnte als Refle-
ion auf diesen Mythos und seine Produktivität verstanden werden: Denn die Infor-
ation, daß sie mit verbundenen Augen entstanden sind, wird in ihnen selbst gleich
ieder zurückgenommen. Jedes Bild weist an seinem unteren Rand einen Text mit
ngaben zu seinem Verfahren aus, doch am Ende soll dieser Text „Lüge“ sein. Der
odernistische Mythos wird unterminiert und zugleich produktiv gemacht.

uch Adorno hat sich für eine bestimmte Form des „mimetischen Verfahrens“ regel-
äßig begeistern können und die Kunst allgemein als „Zuflucht mimetischen Ver-
altens“ bezeichnet: „In ihr stellt das Subjekt, auf wechselnden Stufen seiner Autono-
ie, sich zu einem Anderen, davon getrennt und doch nicht durchaus getrennt.“[03]
s ist das in der Kunst aufscheinende Verhältnis zwischen einem graduell autonomen

04 Vgl. Theodor W. Adorno, Der wunderliche Realist, a.a.O., S. 392.
05 Vgl. ebd., S. 397.
06 Vgl. Theodor W. Adorno, *Ästhetische Theorie*, a.a.O., S. 175.
07 Vgl. Theodor W. Adorno, Die Kunst und die Künste, in: *Gesammelte Schriften 1: Kulturkritik und Gesellschaft*, Frankfurt am Main 1997, S. 432-452, hier S. 448.
08 Vgl. Theodor W. Adorno, *Ästhetische Theorie*, a.a.O., S. 72.

Subjekt und seinem Anderen, das als mimetisches aufgefaßt wird. Adorno bricht mit der klassischen Konzeption von Mimesis als Nachahmung insofern, als es ihm um ein mimetisches Verhalten geht, das nicht etwa nachahmt, sondern einen gleichsam durch sich selbst vorgezeichneten Weg einschlägt. Sein Interesse galt denn auch prinzipiell jenen Künstlern, von denen er glaubte, daß sie sich ihrem Material anschmiegten, sich ihm überließen. Und Kracauer war für Adorno mehr Künstler als Theoretiker. Warum sonst hätte er ihn als „wunderlichen Realisten“ bezeichnet und von seinem Denken in leicht diskreditierender Weise behauptet, daß es mehr Anschauung als Denken – mit anderen Worten „untheoretisch“ gewesen wäre? [04] Kracauers Ergebnisse sagten ihm desto mehr zu, je „blinder sie sich an die Stoffe verloren, welche seine Erfahrung ihm zutrug (...).“ [05] Eine vergleichbare Formulierung findet sich in der *Ästhetischen Theorie*: daß sich ästhetische Rationalität mit „verbundenen Augen“ in die Gestaltung „hineinstürzen“ müsse, „anstatt sie von außen, als Reflexion über das Kunstwerk, zu steuern.“ [06] Das klingt zunächst mystifizierend, den Künstler zum bloßen Vollzugsorgan eines objektiv Gegebenen verklärend und mimetisches Verhalten gegen „Reflexion“ ausspielend, so als handele es sich hier um Gegenpole. Die Sache ist jedoch komplizierter. Denn erstens räumte Adorno wiederholt ein, daß Kunst, um Kunst zu sein, durch das Subjekt hindurchgegangen sein müsse. Das heißt, daß künstlerische Arbeiten zwar durchaus eines Subjektes bedürfen, weil es ihre Objektivität nur als durch das Subjekt vermittelte geben kann. Doch dieses Subjekt, auf das sie angewiesen sind, lassen die Kunstwerke, nachdem sie durch es hindurchgegangen sind, auch hinter sich. Kunstwerke sind bei Adorno die „besseren Subjekte“, und so nützlich es auch erscheint, mit Adorno heute an den „subjektiven Faktor“ zu erinnern, so befremdlich mutet diese Überhöhung an. Zweitens betrachtete er die Kunst als zwischen zwei Polen aufgespannt – zwischen dem eines „einheitsstiftenden, rationalen und eines diffusen, mimetischen Moments“. [07] Als Gegenbegriff zum mimetischen Verhalten könnte man deshalb den der Konstruktion betrachten: Konstruktion ist für Adorno verlängerte subjektive Herrschaft ebenso, wie sie diese einschränkt. Die Konstruktion soll sich quasi-automatisch und notwendig aus der Sache ergeben: „Konstruktion ist nicht Korrektiv oder objektivierende Sicherung des Ausdrucks, sondern muß aus den mimetischen Impulsen ohne Planung gleichsam sich fügen (...).“ [08]

09 Vgl. ebd., S. 92.
10 Vgl. ebd., S. 329.

Kunstwerke, die für Adorno der Rede Wert waren, hatten ein hohes Maß dieser Konstruiertheit aufzuweisen. Was etwas entschieden anderes ist, als wenn sie sich einem vorgegebenen Schema oder einem Regelsystem beugen würden. Auf das von oben her Aufgeprägte oder Aufgezwungene hat Adorno stets allergisch reagiert, was seiner protoavantgardistischen Haltung, einer grundsätzlichen Ablehnung des Überkommenen und Traditionellen geschuldet ist. Daß es durchaus produktiv sein kann, sich ganz bewußt einer gegebenen Konvention zu unterwerfen und daß Künstler/innen möglicherweise nicht umhin können, als sich auf bestimmte Konventionen, die sie natürlich auch ihrerseits gestalten und verändern, zu beziehen, sind Überlegungen, die der Subjektkonzeption Adornos zuwiderlaufen würden. Eine Subjektkonzeption, die dem Subjekt, zumal dem „diskursiv Denkenden", am Ende doch die Souveränität zugesteht, sich über seine Bedingungen zu erheben.

Was hätte Adorno nun zu einer Kunstrichtung wie der Konzeptkunst gesagt, für die die Anfechtung der Idee des Künstlersubjekts ja entscheidend gewesen ist? Wollte man Spekulationen zu dieser Frage anstellen, dann besteht Anlaß zu der Vermutung, daß er jenen konzeptuellen Praktiken der späten sechziger Jahre, die ihre Unterwerfung unter ein System und die Ausstreichung des Subjekts zu ihrem Programm erklärten, eher mit Befremden begegnet wäre. Er hätte ihnen wahrscheinlich vorgeworfen, daß sie nicht mehr als ein bloßes Analogon zur verwalteten Welt seien, rein konstruierte und strikt sachliche Kunstwerke, die vermöge ihrer „Mimesis an die Zweckformen" in ein Kunstgewerbliches übergehen.[09] Dem wäre aus heutiger Sicht entgegenzuhalten, daß die von der Konzeptkunst kultivierte „administrative Ästhetik" (Benjamin Buchloh) eine genuin künstlerische Angelegenheit blieb, deren Sachlichkeit eine überzeichnete und von Irrationalem durchsetzt war und deren „Zwecke" sich von denen der Gesellschaft radikal unterschieden. Spätestens an diesem Punkt könnte Adorno jedoch sein Totschlagargument der mangelnden „Durchgestaltung" aus der Tasche ziehen. Er war skeptisch gegenüber jeglichen Versuchen, sich wie die informelle Malerei dem Kontingenten hinzugeben, was den Künstler von der „Last der Formung"[10] entbinden würde. Einer Kunst, die vorgibt, sich allein dem Zufälligen hinzugeben, vermochte Adorno nicht viel abzugewinnen. Denn der Künstler war für ihn

[11] Vgl. Theodor W. Adorno, Der Artist als Statthalter, in: *Gesammelte Schriften 11, Noten zur Literatur*, Frankfurt am Main 1974, S. 114-126, hier S. 124.
[12] Vgl. Theodor W. Adorno, Zum Gedächtnis Eichendorffs, in: *Noten zur Literatur*, a.a.O., S. 69-94, hier S. 78.
[13] Vgl. Theodor W. Adorno, *Ästhetische Theorie*, a.a.O., S. 63.
[14] Vgl. Theodor W. Adorno, Valérys Abweichungen, in: *Gesammelte Schriften 10.1, Kulturkritik und Gesellschaft I. Prismen. Ohne Leitbild.* S. 181-194, hier S. 190.
[15] Vgl. ebd., S. 188.

ein lenkender Regisseur, jemand, der bewußt über sein Material verfügt und auch die Vorstellung, daß die Menschen zu „bloßen Empfangsapparaten" würden, war für ihn, wie er in einem Text über Valéry implizit zu verstehen gab, alles andere als erstrebenswert.[11] Ich denke, daß er Bretons Ideal der „Registriermaschine" ebensowenig unterschrieben hätte, zu sehr hätte es für ihn nach Kapitulation geklungen; er hätte darin „ästhetische Regression" gewittert. Um so erstaunlicher ist es vor diesem Hintergrund, daß er sich für die *rein rezeptive*, sich den Gegebenheiten anschmiegende Haltung immer wieder stark machen und nachgerade begeistern konnte.

2. Der Künstler als absichtsloser Bergmann?

Es gibt zahlreiche Textstellen, die von dieser Faszination Zeugnis ablegen: angefangen von einem Text über Eichendorffs Dichtung, die Adorno dafür lobt, daß sie sich vom „Strom der Sprache" treiben lasse,[12] vergleichbaren Aussagen („Erfahrungsstrom") zu Proust, bis hin zu einer beiläufigen Bemerkung über „Action Painting" und Aleatorik, bei der die „produktive Funktion nicht imaginierter, überraschender Momente" nicht geleugnet werden könne.[13] Seine Valéry-Rezeption ging in eine ähnliche Richtung, wobei die Methode, für die Valéry gelobt wurde, im Grunde seine eigene war. Mit „unvergleichlicher Autorität", so Adorno über Valéry, habe dieser den objektiven Charakter des Kunstwerks, seine immanente Stimmigkeit und die Zufälligkeit des Subjekts ihr gegenüber dargetan.[14] Mit diesen Worten hätte er auch sein eigenes Anliegen auf den Punkt bringen können. In Valéry sah er einen Vorreiter und Mitstreiter, eine Art „Bruder im Geiste", der den Künstler wie er selbst zum „Vollzugsorgan" seines Materials erklärt: „Der Valérysche Künstler ist ein Bergmann ohne Licht, aber die Schächte und Stollen seines Baus schreiben ihm im Dunkeln die Bewegung vor",[15] so heißt es an einer Stelle, die über Adornos Zustimmung zu diesem Künstlerbild keinen Zweifel läßt. Hat man sich diesen Künstler „als Bergmann ohne Licht" somit als jemanden vorzustellen, der sich vollständig selbst aufgibt, sich blind einer externen Vorgabe überantwortet? Keineswegs. Daß er ohne Licht operiert, heißt im Grunde genommen nur, daß er von keiner Absicht geleitet wird. Adorno war kein Freund der Absicht, schon weil er die Überzeugung vertrat, daß die Sprache über die bloße Intention des Dichters

6 Vgl. Theodor W. Adorno, Parataxis, in: *Noten zur Literatur*, a.a.O., S. 447-491, hier S. 448.
7 Vgl. Peter Laudenbach mit Alexander Kluge: Nur das unsichtbare Bild zählt. Alexander Kluge über den Philosophen Adorno, den 11. September und die Flaschenpost der Kritischen Theorie, in: *Der Tagespiegel*, 11. September 2003, S. 25-26.
8 Vgl. Theodor W. Adorno, *Ästhetische Theorie*, a.a.O., S. 95.0

„hinausschießen" würde. Statt ein ästhetisches Objekt auf Intentionen zu verkürzen, sollte man eher untersuchen, inwieweit es „dem Zwang des Gebildes" gehorchte.[16] Seine Intentionsskepsis war also Folge eines ästhetischen Ansatzes, der sich gegen subjektzentrierte, bei der subjektiven Erfahrung ansetzende Ästhetiken richtete. Er hingegen wollte dem Objekt Vorrang einräumen und es keinesfalls auf subjektive Absichten verkürzt wissen. Von Alexander Kluge stammt eine in diesem Zusammenhang aufschlußreiche Anekdote, die Adornos Intentionsphobie aufs Schönste illustriert: Angesichts eines von Kluge und anderen verfolgten Projekts, einen neunstündigen Film über die Studentenbewegung zu drehen, habe Adorno ihm gesagt, man müsse „blind" filmen.[17] Nur dann, wenn er ohne Absicht etwas aufnehme, würde er etwas aufspüren: „Was das ist, werden Sie erst hinterher sehen." Adorno stellt hier einmal mehr seine Überzeugung unter Beweis, daß es das ästhetische Objekt sei – in diesem Fall die im Film dargestellte Studentenrevolte – dem der Vorrang gebühre, weil es, wie Adorno nicht müde zu sagen wurde, seine eigene Gesetzmäßigkeit besitzt. Somit dürfen sich in ihm auch keine Absichten realisieren.

Diese Vorbehalte gegenüber Intentionen und intentionsbezogenen Erklärungen ziehen sich durch all seine ästhetischen Schriften. Riegls Begriff des Kunstwollens hat er zum Beispiel mit den knappen Worten zurückgewiesen, daß selten das über ein Werk entscheide, was damit gewollt war.[18] Und gegen die „unausrottbare Frage" nach der Intention polemisiert er in seinem Text über Eichendorff, daß diese Frage „gleichgültig" gegenüber dem Komponierten wäre. Intention vermag also Adorno zufolge an das, was künstlerisch geleistet wurde, nicht heranzureichen. Muß man so weit gehen? Ich denke ja und nein. An Adornos Intentionsskepsis heute produktiv anzuknüpfen heißt, die Geltungsmacht von Intention als einer „Letzterklärung" in ihre Schranken zu verweisen. Etwas anderes ist es, ihr jegliche Bedeutung abzusprechen. In Anbetracht der Tatsache jedoch, daß in Teilen der Kunstwelt derzeit eine erstaunliche „Intentionsfixiertheit" zu herrschen scheint, eine Fixierung der Interpreten auf das vermeintlich Beabsichtigte, ließe sich mit Adorno an all jene Aspekte erinnern, die in diesen Absichten eben nicht aufgehen oder über sie hinausschießen. Gerade in den Pressetexten der Kunstinstitutionen finden sich ja regelmäßig Behauptungen wie die, daß künstlerische Arbeiten „Absichten" oder Anliegen hätten, so als würden diese in oder von ihnen

[19] Vgl. Marcel Duchamp, *Der Kreative Akt. Duchampagne brut*, Hamburg 1991, S. 11f.

umgesetzt. Dort treibt Intentionsfixiertheit ihre Blüten. Die Zähigkeit solch intentionsbezogener Erklärungen hat meines Erachtens damit zu tun, daß sie die Kunst scheinbar „überzeugend" – nämlich mit der Individualität des Künstlers – wegerklären. Eine mögliche Folge dieser „Intentionsfixiertheit" für das Selbstverständnis der Künstler/innen wäre noch darin zu sehen, daß sich viele von ihnen heute dazu angehalten sehen, ihr Anliegen in möglichst klaren Worten schriftlich zu formulieren, und zwar in einer Weise, die oft etwas Rechtfertigendes an sich hat. Das sind Erscheinungen, die sich mit Mißverständnissen in der Rezeption der Konzeptkunst erklären. Was einmal der programmatische Versuch der Konzeptkunst war, Kunst zu entmystifizieren und als nüchterne Beschreibung eines Vorhabens neu zu bestimmen – wobei diese „Pläne" rückblickend betrachtet reichlich idiosynkratisch anmuten und keinen Zweifel an ihrer Stilisiertheit lassen –, ist heute zur trüben Konvention pressetextartiger Absichtserklärungen geronnen. So als wäre Kunst eine Mittel-Zweck-Beziehung und der Künstler ein sich selbst transparentes Subjekt, das seine Vorhaben schlicht künstlerisch „umsetzt".

3. Kein Ende der Strategie

Dabei hatte bereits Marcel Duchamp die Vorstellung, daß in der Kunst etwas vom Künstler Beabsichtigtes ausgedrückt würde, mit seinem „persönlichen Kunst-Koeffizienten" den Wind aus den Segeln genommen. Dieser Koeffizient sei, so lautete seine mit wissenschaftlicher Seriosität kokettierende Formel, als eine „arithmetische Relation zwischen dem Unausgedrückten-aber-Beabsichtigten und dem Unabsichtlich-Ausgedrückten" zu verstehen.[19] Das heißt mit anderen Worten, daß das Ausgedrückte nicht unbedingt das ist, was beabsichtigt wurde und umgekehrt das Beabsichtigte in der Regel unausgedrückt bleibt. Diese Zuspitzung hätte Adorno sicherlich gefallen, zumal sie Intention auf eine Weise relativiert, die auf ihre Aushöhlung hinausläuft. Den Geltungsbereich der Intention auf diese Weise einzuschränken, muß jedoch meines Erachtens *nicht* zwangsläufig bedeuten, daß man das Kind sogleich mit dem Bade ausschüttet und sich von dem in den achtziger Jahren aufgekommenen und in den neunziger Jahren durchgesetzten Bild des *strategisch* operierenden, also eben durchaus

Absichten verfolgenden Künstlers zugunsten des „absichtslosen“ verabschiedet. Auch wenn man auf den ersten Blick meinen könnte, daß beide Künstlerbilder – strategischer und absichtsloser Künstler – nur schwer miteinander zu vereinbaren wären. Ich würde hingegen vorschlagen, die ja die Handlungs- und Interventionsmöglichkeiten des Künstlers anerkennende Idee der „künstlerischen Strategie“ dahingehend zu präzisieren, daß man zunächst einmal – ganz in Adornos Sinne – bei den künstlerischen Arbeiten selbst ansetzt und untersucht, wie sie Strategien aufführen respektive wie diese in ihnen aufgeführt werden. Und bei dieser Gelegenheit würde man zu der Feststellung gelangen, daß sich künstlerische Arbeiten darin keineswegs erschöpfen. Mehr noch: Die „Strategie“, deren Ausdruck künstlerische Arbeiten auch sind oder *sein können*, muß nicht unbedingt deckungsgleich mit dem sein, was der Künstler strategisch zu wollen meint oder zu wollen vorgibt. In dem Moment, wo sich die mit dem Begriff der künstlerischen Strategie verbundene Vorstellung des über sich selbst verfügenden Künstlersubjekts als eine Fiktion erweist, wird es mithin möglich, den strategisch operierenden Künstler anders zu bestimmen. Auf Adorno kann man dafür allerdings nicht zurückgreifen, weil sein Subjektideal dem ebenso diametral entgegensteht wie besagte Intentionsphobie. Ging er doch von einem starken Subjekt aus, das nicht nur dazu in der Lage sein sollte, sich den Gegebenheiten anzuschmiegen, sondern auch die richtigen Konsequenzen aus ihnen zu ziehen hatte. So mußte der besagte „Bergmann ohne Licht“ eben auch die Fähigkeit besitzen, das, was die Schächte und Stollen ihm scheinbar objektiv vorschreiben, überhaupt zu erkennen; sich dieser „Forderung“ entsprechend verhalten.

4. Das Problem der richterlichen Verfügung

Das zentrale Problem von Adornos Ästhetik sind ihre regulativen Ideen: Vom „Material“ zum Beispiel sollen bestimmte Forderungen so ausgehen, als seien diese von vornherein gegeben. Das ist aber auch der Preis, den er für seine normative Ästhetik bezahlt, die auf der Basis bestimmter Annahmen Urteile fällt. Auf der einen Seite gibt es den Künstler, der mimetischen Impulsen nachgebend einer „objektiven“ Forderung entsprechen soll, und auf der anderen Seite das mimetisch funktionierende Kunstwerk,

[20] Theodor W. Adorno, *Ästhetische Theorie*, a.a.O., S. 159.

das gleichsam zu sich selbst findet, das „sich selbst gleich macht“: „Die Mimesis der Kunstwerke ist Ähnlichkeit mit sich selbst.“ [20] Das Kunstwerk zielt also nicht darauf, etwas einem anderen nachzumachen, sondern darauf, sich selbst ähnlich zu werden. Dieses „Selbst“ des Kunstwerks scheint nun seinerseits von vornherein gegeben zu sein, so als wäre jedem Kunstwerk sein eigenes ästhetisches Ideal bereits eingeschrieben, dem es nur nachzukommen hätte. Und der Künstler wäre dann derjenige, der nur noch dafür zu sorgen hat, daß das Kunstwerk diesen Weg zu sich selbst findet – eine zweifache Fiktion, die neben Adorno nur noch Clement Greenberg auf vergleichbare Weise produktiv gemacht hat. Damit sie funktioniert, bedarf es eines Betrachters, der am Ende doch wieder über große Autorität verfügt, auf dessen subjektive Einschätzung es nämlich ankommt. Nicht nur muß er grundsätzlich zum Nachvollzug befähigt und Kenner jener „immanenten Gesetzlichkeit“ sein, mehr noch stattet ihn dieser „immanente Nachvollzug“, der als ein mimetischer Prozeß aufgefaßt wird, gleichsam automatisch mit der Fähigkeit aus, das Objekt an seinem ästhetischen Ideal zu messen und darüber zu entscheiden, ob es erreicht wurde. Die Konsequenzen, die sich aus diesem Postulat des privilegierten, weil zur mimetischen Einfühlung befähigten Betrachters ergeben, werden bei Adorno allerdings nicht erörtert. Meines Wissens hat er kaum über die Voraussetzungen, die ihn selbst zu dieser Form der „angemessenen“ Rezeption befähigten, nachgedacht. Die Figur des „immanenten Nachvollzugs“ ist auch insofern problematisch, als sie einen unmittelbaren Zugang und ein nahtloses Aufnehmen suggeriert, was es so natürlich nicht gibt, nicht zuletzt deshalb, weil es die performative Leistung des Betrachters ignoriert. Dessen Wahrnehmung ist ja grundsätzlich vermittelt; von Projektionen und Verkennungen durchzogen.
In diesem Szenario muß auch der Künstler auf der Höhe seiner Arbeit sein, die von ihr angeblich ausgehenden Forderungen unmittelbar in sich aufnehmen. Dies führt zur Annahme eines gegebenen „Standes“ des Materials, was in der Konsequenz bedeutete, daß bestimmte Vorgehensweisen hinter diesen „Stand“ zurückfielen, während sich andere mit ihm auf Augenhöhe befinden sollten. So war die figurative Malerei für Adorno, die ja die Darstellung des Menschen und seine Repräsentierbarkeit voraussetzt, definitiv an ihr Ende gekommen. Heute würde man sagen, daß nicht die figurative Malweise generell das Problem sein kann, sondern eher schon eine spezifische Form

1 Theodor W. Adorno, *Ästhetische Theorie*, a.a.O., S. 175.
2 Vgl. Isabelle Graw: Der fleckige Boden des Ateliers. Über die neuen Bilder von Christopher Wool, in: *Texte zur Kunst*, Nr. 49, März 2003, S. 168-171.

des künstlerischen Umgangs mit ihr. Es ist durchaus denkbar, überzeugend für die figurativen Bilder von Alex Katz zu argumentieren und zugleich dem Werk von Lucian Freud mit Skepsis zu begegnen. Nur – um produktiv über aktuelle kunsttheoretische Probleme nachdenken zu können, ist es gar nicht nötig, den ganzen Weg zu gehen und Adornos Postulate bedingungslos zu unterschreiben. Man kann auf halbem Wege stehenbleiben.

5. Dem folgen, wohin es die Hand zieht

„Dem folgen, wohin es die Hand zieht" – das war für Adorno „Mimesis als Vollstreckung der Objektivität."[21] Wobei sich Objektivität an der Richtung festmacht, in die es die Hand angeblich zieht. Eine Richtung, die von vornherein gegeben sein soll. Einmal abgesehen von diesem, seiner normativen Ästhetik geschuldeten Problem, steht dieses Postulat in erster Linie für seine *Anerkennung eines mimetischen Prinzips* in der Kunst, und von diesem Prinzip würde ich sagen, daß es von der Kunsttheorie lange Zeit zu Unrecht vernachlässigt wurde. In den letzten Jahren ist man zwar verstärkt dazu übergegangen, der Kunst ihre Eigengesetzlichkeit und „relative Autonomie" zuzugestehen. Doch dieses Zugeständnis blieb weitgehend abstrakt und schematisch, ohne daß man den konkreten Schauplatz dieser Eigengesetzlichkeit in den künstlerischen Arbeiten selbst ausgemacht hätte. Von Adornos These der Kunst als „Zuflucht mimetischen Verhaltens" ausgehend, läßt sich nun der Ort, wo Eigengesetzlichkeit und Fremdbestimmtheit ineinandergreifen, konkreter bestimmen. Dieser Ort ist das mimetische Prinzip – es steht für eine eigenwillige, unvorhersehbare Dynamik ebenso wie für die Orientierung an einem Anderen. Die Bilder von Christopher Wool können hier als Beispiel dienen, weil sie ihre Verstrickung in mimetische, quasi-automatische Prozesse selbst vorführen und zugleich den Beweis dafür antreten, daß sich aus der Entscheidung für eine bestimmte Technik, in diesem Fall ein rudimentäres Siebdruckverfahren, bestimmte Konsequenzen ergeben, eine durch das Siebdruckverfahren losgetretene Dynamik, der der Künstler nur noch Folge zu leisten scheint.[22] Zugleich hat er natürlich die Entscheidung für diese Versuchsanordnung getroffen, sich bereit gehalten und gewisse Vorkehrungen dafür getroffen, daß der Prozeß, dem er nun anscheinend nur

[23] Vgl. Theodor W. Adorno, Zum Gedächtnis Eichendorffs, in: *Noten zur Literatur*, a.a.O., S. 69-94, hier S. 79.
[24] Vgl. ebd., S. 84.

noch beiwohnt, in eine bestimmte Richtung hin verläuft. Für die Überführung dieses Sachverhalts in eine Produktionsästhetik ist Adornos mimetische Konzeption von großem Nutzen. Er ging ja von einem auf ähnliche Weise zur „passiven Aktivität" befähigten Künstler aus, setzte jedoch ein inzwischen fragwürdig gewordenes „starkes Subjekt" voraus. Was nämlich zunächst nach Selbstaufgabe, Selbstausstreichung und einem vollständigen Sich-Überlassen geklungen hatte, ist am Ende doch auf ein „starkes Subjekt" angewiesen. So wird Eichendorff von Adorno eine „Suspension des Ichs" attestiert, ein Ich, das sich an das „chaotisch sich Andrängende" der Sprache preisgeben würde.[23] Doch der Dichter muß eben auch „stark" genug sein, um diese Kraft zur Schwäche überhaupt aufbringen zu können, um mithin zu einer Schwäche zu gelangen, die dem Sprachgefälle nicht länger widersteht: „... das ist das Gefälle der Sprache, das, *wohin sie von sich aus möchte* (Hervorhebung von mir), die Kraft des Dichters aber die zur Schwäche, die, dem Sprachgefälle nicht zu widerstehen, eher als die, es zu meistern."[24] Es bedarf also einer gewissen „Kraft", sich der bei Adorno als gegeben vorausgesetzten Richtung, in die einen die Sprache angeblich zieht, zu überlassen.

Angesichts derartiger Erkentnisse könnte man nun zu Recht fragen, was an ihnen heute eigentlich kunstheoretisch relevant sein soll? Zumal sie auf den ersten Blick in einer Subjekt-Objekt-Dichotomie verhaftet bleiben? Ist es nicht banal, zu sagen, daß es zur Schwäche einer gewissen Stärke bedarf? Keineswegs. Denn noch für die vermeintlich subjektfeindlichste künstlerische Praxis wird man irgendwann einräumen müssen, daß das Subjekt in ihr seine Spuren hinterließ. Die *Appropriation Art* der achtziger Jahre ist hierfür ein gutes Beispiel, zumal sie vom Mythos der Subjektkritik zehrte. Man ging davon aus, daß es in ihr nicht auf die subjektive Gestaltung, sondern auf die jeweils appropriierte Vorlage ankäme. Kunst sollte sich – wie der Name schon sagt – allein über ihre Aneignung definieren. Betrachtet man jedoch die frühen Arbeiten von Sherrie Levine, jene wiederfotografierten Fotos von Walker Evans zum Beispiel, durch die sie zu einer der bekanntesten Vertreterinnen dieser Praxisform avancierte, dann wird man feststellen, daß diese Arbeiten eben doch eines Subjektes bedürfen, eines Subjektes mithin, das bestimmte Entscheidungen trifft, etwa die für eine bestimmte Form der Rahmung oder die für eine Versuchsanordnung, die dieses Subjekt für Externes (das

5 Vgl. Isabelle Graw: Sublime Aneignung. Sherrie Levine, in: Dies.: *Die bessere Hälfte. Künstlerinnen des 20. und 21. Jahrhunderts*, Köln 2003, S. 48-50.

zu Appropriierende) öffnet und ansprechbar macht.[25] Die Frage also, wie das Subjekt „eintritt", scheint mir für die unterschiedlichsten künstlerischen Praxisformen – von der *écriture automatique* bis hin zur *Appropriation Art* – untersuchenswert zu sein. Hinzu kommt, daß Adorno mit seiner Konzeption von Kunst als einem mimetischen Verfahren die starre Gegenüberstellung von Subjekt und Objekt ohnehin aufgebrochen hat, denn zwischen dem Künstler, der sich seinem Gegenstand anschmiegt, und diesem Gegenstand selbst sind ja keine klaren Grenzen mehr zu ziehen.

6. Am Schreibtisch

Warum verfiel Adorno auf die Wiederbelebung der romantischen Vorstellung, daß die Sprache einen wie von selbst in eine bestimmte Richtung ziehe? Neben seinem Bedürfnis, dem ästhetischen Objekt Gerechtigkeit widerfahren zu lassen, gibt es, denke ich, noch eine andere Erklärung. Er schrieb, wie so oft, eine subjektive Erfahrung (die des Schreibenden) dem Objekt (der Sprache) zu. Wer schreibt, weiß gewöhnlich von dieser Erfahrung zu berichten, daß man meint, von der Sprache gezogen zu werden, von einem Satz zum nächsten gleitend. Es spricht, es schreibt, man wird geschrieben. Aus diesem „subjektiven Empfinden" nun, das phantasmatische Züge trägt, hat Adorno eine gegebene Richtung der Sprache abgeleitet. Für eine Produktionsästhetik ist sein mimetisches Postulat gleichwohl von Bedeutung. Denn für die produktionsästhetische Perspektive ist es ja durchaus relevant, festzustellen, daß der Schreibende (oder Komponierende) zu Beginn oft nicht weiß, wohin ihn seine Sprache führt. Auch Gliederungen vermögen diese Unvorhersehbarkeiten nicht auszuräumen, und Strukturpläne zeichnen sich ja gewöhnlich dadurch aus, daß sie unablässig verworfen und den Entwicklungen angepaßt werden. Eine neue Fragestellung kann ganz unverhofft auftauchen, sich aus zunächst nebensächlich erscheinenden Überlegungen ergeben. So mag es dem Produzenten tatsächlich so vorkommen, als sei es die Sprache selbst, die ihm die Richtung weist. Der Adorno-Leser sieht sich übrigens einem vergleichbaren Effekt ausgesetzt. Noch ehe er sich versieht, ist er beim Adorno-Lesen in ein Denken eingetaucht, von dem er mitgezogen wird. Adorno läßt den Leser am Prozeßhaften seines Denkens teilnehmen. Je weiter man sich beispielsweise in der *Ästhetischen*

[26] Vgl. Britta Scholze, *Kunst als Kritik. Adornos Weg aus der Dialektik*, Würzburg 2000, S. 105

Theorie vorarbeitet, desto intensiver taucht man in dieses Denken ein, abrupte Wendungen und Sprünge eingeschlossen. Hat man sich einmal auf diese Lektüre eingelassen, dann ist man auch schon Teil von ihr und Mitverfechter eines Denkens, zu dem eben auch paradoxe Formulierungen und aporetische Konstruktionen gehören. Man liest sich ein, gewöhnt sich an den Sound, so daß vormals befremdlich anmutende Formulierungen plötzlich evident erscheinen. Die mimetische Einfühlung kann bis zur Übernahme bestimmter Manierismen gehen. Aus einem mimetischen Sich-Anschmiegen wird Einverleibung. Adornos Schreiben hat in der Tat etwas Ansteckendes. Darauf, daß er selbst in hohem Maße einverleibend gearbeitet hat, hat kürzlich Britta Scholze hingewiesen, indem sie die *Ästhetische Theorie* treffend als „Durchgang durch die Kategorien idealistischer Ästhetik" charakterisierte – ein Durchgang mithin, bei dem er sich Übernahmen leistete, ohne das Übernommene jedes Mal auszuweisen.[26]

7. Autonomie und Heteronomie

Diese „Kategorien idealistischer Ästhetik" aufzugreifen bedeutete allerdings auch, sie gegen den Strich zu bürsten, sie auszuklopfen, wie einen staubigen Teppich, bei dem man nachsieht, ob er überhaupt noch verwertbar ist. Auf mimetische Weise etwas zu übernehmen war für Adorno gleichbedeutend mit „kritisch" dagegen Stellung beziehen. Mimesis besaß für ihn eine kritische Funktion – mit dem mimetischen Sich-Anschmiegen sollte ein kritischer Anspruch verknüpft sein. Dieser Umschlag von Mimesis in Kritik gleicht einem magischen Vorgang, bei dem die „Mimesis ans Verhärtete und Entfremdete" oder die „Mimesis ans Tote" bereits gleichbedeutend mit „Kritik" sein soll. Eine Hoffnung, der die Erfahrung mit Gegenwartskunst entgegenzuhalten wäre, die sie nicht bestätigt und vielmehr zeigt, daß mit einem solchen Automatismus keineswegs zu rechnen ist. Weder die künstlerische Strategie der Affirmation, die für Künstler wie Jeff Koons oder Haim Steinbach in den achtziger Jahren in Anschlag gebracht wurde, noch die heute vielbeschworenen „Überbietungstechniken" sind automatisch kritisch. Eine künstlerische Arbeit, in der die Verhältnisse auf die Spitze getrieben werden, hat sie deshalb noch lange nicht kritisiert. Der Film *Capital* von Sarah Morris beispielsweise hat zwar zweifellos die kapitalistischen Verhältnisse

isuell zu übertreffen versucht, sie in einer Art Mikrostudie auseinandergenommen ind vorgeführt. Ihn deshalb als Kapitalismuskritik zu lesen, wäre jedoch überzogen.)ie Vorstellung, daß eine künstlerische Arbeit Kritik üben könne, scheint mir ohne-iin fragwürdig zu sein. Denn wo und wie genau sollte diese eigentlich statthaben? /ersteht man Kritik im geläufigen Sinne als eine Fehler und Versäumnisse beanstan-lende Stellungnahme, dann vermögen künstlerische Arbeiten nur in Ausnahmefällen - etwa im Frühwerk von Hans Haacke – Kritik zu leisten. Und „Kritik" ist auch hier ils künstlerische ausgewiesen und nur ein Aspekt unter vielen.
Es scheint mir deshalb sinnvoller, mit und gegen Adorno von einem heteronomen Kunstwerk auszugehen, das von fremden Gesetzen bestimmt ist, diese aber auch auto-10m entwirft, gestaltet und sich gegebenenfalls zu ihnen verhält. Dies läuft darauf iinaus, Adornos nicht-restriktiven Autonomiebegriff konsequent zu Ende zu denken. Er hat ja unausgesetzt Nachweise für die Eigengesetzlichkeit der Kunst erbracht, ohne ie in eine abgeschlossene Sondersphäre verbannen zu wollen. In einer berühmt gewor-lenen Formulierung ist von ihrem Doppelcharakter die Rede – *fait social* und auto-10mes Gebilde zugleich. Kunst als „mimetisches Verfahren" zu begreifen, läuft nicht iur auf die Anerkennung, sondern auf die Veranschaulichung dieses Doppelcharak-ters hinaus. Denn das mimetische Verfahren folgt einer eigenen Dynamik, die sich zu-gleich an bestimmten Vorgaben orientiert. Doch wie genau treten gesellschaftliche Zwänge in die Kunst ein? Es ist das Material, dem bei Adorno dieser Schritt aufgebür-det wird. Es schleppt Gesellschaft gleichsam mit und folgt zugleich seiner eigenen Logik. Dieser Ansatz scheint mir auch für die Analyse zeitgenössischer künstlerischer Praktiken nützlich zu sein. Mit der Entscheidung für ein bestimmtes Material – so etwa dem bedruckten und bestickten Stoff als Träger eines Bildes von Cosima von Bonin –, wird die künstlerische Arbeit heteronom. Denn mit dem Material werden der künstlerischen Arbeit externe Zwänge aufgeladen: so zum Beispiel die Geschichte der jüngsten künstlerischen Verwendung von Stoffen (die Linie Polke-Palermo), damit einhergehende Ansprüche und Interpretationen, mit denen zu rechnen ist. Mit der Ent-scheidung für ein Stoffbild handelt sich der Künstler gleichsam automatisch einen Referenzrahmen ein, der sich nicht abschütteln läßt, so wie bei Adorno der Schein. Die Bedeutung des Stoffes ist dabei stets als historisch spezifisch anzusehen: Zu einem

bestimmten Zeitpunkt und innerhalb einer bestimmten künstlerischen Formation ist der Stoff auf bestimmte Weise kodiert. Es ist natürlich durchaus möglich, dies zu ignorieren, diesen Bedeutungen den Rücken zuzukehren. Zeitgenössische Praktiken zeichnen sich in der Regel dadurch aus, daß sie mit diesen Codes umgehen, ein Bewußtein von ihnen signalisieren, sie reflektieren. Aber nicht nur. Heteronom sind sie nicht nur auf dieser materiellen Ebene, sondern auch in bezug auf ihren ökonomischen Status. Sie sind heteronom aufgrund ihrer nicht tot zu kriegenden Warenförmigkeit. Kunstwerke sind am Ende reine Tauschwerte, und wer Kunst produziert, hat sich unweigerlich in diesen Tauchwertcharakter seiner Arbeit, mithin in den Kunstmarkt verstrickt. Wobei es natürlich unterschiedliche Weisen geben kann, sich zu diesem Kunstmarkt zu verhalten. Diese Heteronomie der Kunst ist heute zweifellos viel ausgeprägter als noch zu Adornos Zeiten, dem Kunstmarkt und Kulturindustrie prinzipiell verdächtig waren. Ich denke jedoch, daß diese weitgehende Fremdbestimmtheit kultureller Produkte ihrer relativen Eigengesetzlichkeit keinen Abbruch tut. Kunst ist heteronom und vermag zu der Bedingung dieser Heteronomie auch Autonomien auszubilden. Am Beispiel des mimetischen Verfahrens läßt sich dies besonders gut demonstrieren. Gerade derjenige Künstler, der mimetisch verfährt, verschreibt sich ja einerseits einer eigenwilligen Dynamik, die andererseits von einer externen Vorgabe nachgerade eingefordert wird.

[01] Theodor W. Adorno, Jene zwanziger Jahre, in: *Eingriffe. Neun kritische Modelle,* Frankfurt am Main 1963, S. 59-68, hier S. 59.

ENE NEUNZIGER JAHRE

Georg Schöllhammer

chlagworte machen sich verdächtig nicht bloß durch ihre Funktion, den Gedanken ur Spielmarke zu degradieren; sie sind der Index ihrer eigenen Unwahrheit. Theodor W. Adorno)[01]

Nicht ganz selten passiert es, daß die letzte Generation eines im Erblassen begriffenen ntellektuellen Paradigmas ihre Texte zu einer manierierten und brillanten Präsenz ringt. Sie ist im Stande, die Rivalen von einst in ihr Denken mit einzubeziehen, sie in hm wirken zu lassen. Sie koaliert mit den ehedem fremden Argumenten, die von den igenen jetzt friedlich umschlossen sind. Texte entstehen so, die gegen die fremde Welt iner neuen methodisch frischen, rauhen, von einer anderen Basis aus denkenden Generation noch einmal brillant Position zu beziehen vermögen.
n einer im Umfang schmalen Betrachtung, die dem Kunsthändler und Theoretiker des Kubismus, Daniel-Henry Kahnweiler, gewidmet ist, bedenkt Theodor W. Adorno 1963 ie Konjunktur einer Nostalgie. Der kleine und glossenhafte Essay hat den Titel „Jene wanziger Jahre" und wendet sich gegen die im Kunstbetrieb bis heute gängige Dezenienlogik von Epochengeschichte. Adorno reklamiert in diesem preziosen Stück die roduktionsgeschichte von ästhetischen Ideen weg von ihrer Durchsetzung im Mainstream zurück in die zwar von Ungewißheiten und Marginalisierungen, jedoch von ünstlerischer Aufbruchstimmung gezeichnete, rauhe Zeit, in der sich ein ästhetisches aradigma in den nachmaligen Eliten zu befestigen beginnt. Und er macht in diesem ext noch eine andere Wendung, die fast paradigmenhaft für seinen Pessimismus gegenber dem Mainstream steht: Er zeichnet das Populäre, die Einverständniskultur mit em Exaltierten, welche in einer Oberflächenlektüre die Zwanziger Jahre-Nostalgie für ne auch nicht gerade befreiten Frühsechziger so spannend erscheinen ließ, als falsche Nostalgie. In Wirklichkeit, sagt Adorno, sei gerade schon in den zwanziger Jahren jenes atale nicht mehr Weiterarbeiten an Motiven des Vorkriegsaufbruchs geschehen, sei as Prekäre der Moderne gegen einen Entertainment-Mainstream getauscht worden. Hinter dessen frei gedacht scheinenden Fassaden habe schon die Vorbereitung zur päteren Liquidierung der eigentlichen Potentiale des Schwierigen und Nonkonformen ich ereignet, mit welchen die Kultur der Avantgarden der späten Jahrhundertwende en bürgerlichen Konsensus spätimpressionistischer Seinsvergewisserung verlassen hatte:

02 Ebd., S. 61f.

die Liquidierung, wie sie seit 1930 statt hatte. 1930 sei schon 1920 angelegt gewesen. Adorno weist 1963 noch einmal auf die Moderne der 1910er Jahre zurück. Sie sei die Verliererin dieses Konsums der Dezennien, sie habe sich nach der Katastrophe des Nazismus und des 2. Weltkrieges wegen ihrer stilistischen und formalistischen Strenge und deren Verdrehung im Mainstream der zwanziger Jahre als nicht weiter gedachtes Fragment erwiesen. Das Projekt einer neuen Ästhetik müsse daher als abgebrochen und verdrängt, verquer und verwunden gelten und sei schwer wieder zu installieren. Schon die Kunstgeschichte des Jahrhundertanfangs könne also nur als Folge von Verwerfungen, Diskontinuitäten, Brüchen und falschen Anschlüssen gedacht und geschrieben werden.
„Trotzdem hat die Vorstellung von den zwanziger Jahren als der Welt, in der man, wie es in Brechts *Mahagony* heißt, alles dürfen darf, als einer Utopie auch ihr Wahres. Damals sah es wie die Möglichkeit einer politisch befreiten Gesellschaft aus. Allerdings sah es bloß so aus.“ [02]

Theorie usw.
Anfang der neunziger Jahre war es im Kunstbetrieb Westeuropas recht modisch zu sagen, die kulturelle Welt sei eine politische. Gesagt wurde das ganz generell und wohl auch vor dem Hintergrund der neuen sich abzeichnenden politischen wie kulturellen Geographien nach dem Zusammenbruch des sozialistischen Imperiums und vor dem Wachwerden eines anderen Produktionsmodus am Proszenium des aus Installation, Malerei und Objekt sowie bestenfalls Videoinstallation bestehenden Genretheaters der Kunst der achtziger Jahre – dem Wachwerden dessen, was später Neue Medien hieß. Solche Gefügeverschiebungen, wie sie sich damals abzeichneten und wie sie ja dann tatsächlich von etwa 1987 an über die folgenden Jahre in den Kunstbetrieb eingeschrieben wurden, werden im intellektuellen und im künstlerischen Leben oft von Latenzen begleitet. Vor allem wenn sich eine materielle Basis für den Diskurs von einer anderen abgelöst sieht, beziehungsweise wie Ende der achtziger Jahre in einer Krise befindet (diesmal war das der Kunstmarkt).
Damals ereignete sich ein solcher Sprung, der auf Latenzen fiel. Eine Art Umkehrung von Adornos pessimistischer Zwanziger Jahre-Analyse fand statt. Junge KünstlerInnen

ezogen sich wieder auf abgebrochene, nicht kanonisierte oder ausagierte Motive polisch-konzeptueller Kunst der späten sechziger und frühen siebziger Jahre, versuchten trategien aus der vom postmodernen *Horror Conceptui* und seinen Materialschlachten erdeckten lokalen Szene zu rekonstruieren und weiter zu denken.

)ie Verdrängungsgeschichten, mit welchen diese Arbeit sich konfrontiert sah, wurden twa so skizziert: Anfang der siebziger Jahre begann sich in den ersten großen Kabeletzen der europäischen audiovisuellen Medien jene Zersplitterung der Diskurse zu inallieren, auf der dann die europäische und zuallererst französische Theorie der „Postoderne" ihre Kritikmuster aufbaute. Spätestens ab Mitte der siebziger Jahre beseitigte er „postmoderne" Medienkapitalismus die Dogmen der 68er-Auseinandersetzung nit Faschismus, Kolonialismus, Kapitalismus und Unterdrückung. Oder er bediente sich rer für seine Gesellschaftspolitik, wertete sie um in einen zynischen sozialdarwinisschen Neoliberalismus. Ein Beispiel: Franco Basaglia und seine konsequent aus der manzipatorischen Linken entwickelte De-Hospitalisierungspolitik sogenannter Geistesranker in der Klinik von Triest, ein radikalreformerisches Konzept, bewirkte aus dem eist von 68 in den siebziger Jahren die Schließung sämtlicher geschlossener psychiaischer Anstalten per Gesetz in ganz Italien. Ein weltweit bestauntes Modell. Ronald eagan bewirkte mit seiner radikalen Kürzung der Gesundheits- und Sozialbudgets in en achtziger Jahren in den USA eine beinahe ebenso konsequente De-Hospitalisierung, ie die Leute aus der Klinik auf die Straße warf.

n der kritischen europäischen und US-amerikanischen Kunst der siebziger bis frühen chtziger Jahre bedeutete, das Subjektive gegen den Hintergrund dieser emergenten lediokratisierung und Ökonomisierung der Welt darzustellen – wie das auch Deleuze nd Guattari gefordert hatten –, eben auch Selbst-, oder eben Geschlechts-, Rassenewußtsein auszustellen. Es bedeutete auch, Sozialisation als keineswegs beliebige gellschaftliche Formung, sondern als einen Prozeß der Auseinandersetzung zwischen em Wunschpotential des Individuums und den Institutionen und Medien als Verkörerung gesellschaftlicher Vorstellungen zu betonen. Michel Foucault hatte noch gehofft, s existiere ein gleichsam unbeschriebener Körper, gleichzeitig aber in seinen Arbeiten chlagend klargemacht, daß es keine Rückkehr zu einem Modell des Körpers gibt – nd damit natürlich auch zu keinem Modell des Subjektes –, das nicht schon immer

von kulturellen Bedeutungen interpretiert ist. Das war der Status quo. Gerade auf dies Differenz zwischen einer kulturellen Produktion, in der die ProduzentInnen sich beobachten und auf ihre Standards und Erfolgsbewertungen achtgeben, zu jener, die sic auf die der Publika, also auf etwas schon immer anderswo Interpretiertes und Repräsentiertes berufen muß, weist auch Adorno in seinem Essay hin. Ihm geht es darum zu unterscheiden, um genau jene Bruchstelle zu zeigen. Die Bruchstelle zwischen: au der einen Seite der Kultur als der Auseinandersetzung mit der Kontrolle über die Machtapparate des kulturellen Feldes, und auf der anderen Seite der distinkten Zahl jener Strategien und Artefakte einer wesentlich als neu verstandenen Kunst, die von jenen produziert und praktiziert werden, die um andere Netzwerke kämpfen, Netzwerke, welche ihre eigenen Techniken und Tropen, Formen und Argumente haben.

Daher stellt sich die Frage: Was wollten wir also sagen, als wir Ende der achtziger Jahre wieder sagten, daß die Kunst nichts als ein soziales Konstrukt sei? Von wo au konnten wir das sagen? Es gab keinen sicheren Boden für Kritik, und das genau sollte mit unserer Kritik ausgedrückt werden: daß klar war, das es keinen sicheren Boden fü Kritik gibt. Die Gefahr kam nicht aus der Richtung eines zu starken Glaubens an ideologische Argumente, die für Tatsachen gehalten wurden, sondern sie erschien in Form eines ungeheuren Mißtrauens in Tatsachen, die als ideologische Wendungen mißverstanden wurden.
Wenn viele im Kunstbetrieb heute – und eben ganz anders als Anfang der neunziger Jahre – solche Schwierigkeiten damit haben, sich Kategorien wie institutionelle Bedeutung und politische Interpretation als die Schlüsselprobleme kultureller Analyse vor zustellen, und die Kategorie Kultur vor allem wieder vor dem Hintergrund ökonomischer Prozesse gelesen wird, hängt das wohl damit zusammen. Es liegt eine gewiss historische Ironie in der gegenwärtigen Hofierung der Zentralität von Theorie, Ökonomie und Zirkulation für die Analyse von Kultur. Wenn eine Position die intellektuell Welt dominiert, ist das meist keine Zeit der Kreativität, sondern eine der Stagnation, die Zeit einer Orthodoxie, welche nur selten mehr kreativ ist. Das scheint mir jetzt ge rade der Fall zu sein.
Natürlich ist das Momentum, die Zeit der Theorie nicht verloren, nicht vorbei, doch

sind die Theoriemaschinen, um einen Begriff von Deleuze abzuwandeln, oft gänzlich unproportional zu ihrem Subjekt geworden. Nein, es ist etwas anderes, das man hier sagen könnte: Das Wort Theorie ist im Kunstbetrieb zum Codewort für relativ leicht vorhersagbare Positionen verfallen. Tritt das Wort auf, werden meistens Ideen von sozialer Transformation, historischer Agency, die – wie immer verstandene – Disposition des Selbst, die Heterogenität von Kulturen, ein wenig Lacanistische Analyse des Symbolischen und knappe Post-Empire-Globalisierungsanalysen mit ihr geliefert etc. Alles das ist zudem im Kontext einer ranzig-spätaufklärerischen Gedankenwelt vorgetragen.

Militärische Planungsstäbe werden oft beschuldigt, mit ihren aktuellen Strategien einen Krieg zu spät dran zu sein, die Zeit nicht zu sehen. Es ist lange her, seit Intellektuelle und KünstlerInnen an der Spitze der Ereignisse standen. Auch die Intellektuellen schienen Anfang der neunziger Jahre eine Auseinandersetzung zu spät dran zu sein, eine Auseinandersetzung verpaßt zu haben. Wie der Modernismus, auf den sich die Kritik der sechziger Jahre bezog, schon seine Krisen hatte, war auch die Zeit der Reaktion auf die Krisensymptome der postmodernen achtziger Jahre Anfang der neunziger Jahre schon vorbei. Daher war es wohl auch alles andere als ein Zufall, daß jene Arbeiten, in denen im wesentlichen das gesamte Repertoire künstlerischer Ausdrucksmöglichkeiten angelegt war, auf die sich die kritische Kunst der späten achtziger Jahre bezog, genau zwischen Berkeley 64, also Hippieculture und Black Panthers, Paris 1968, also intellektuelle Revolte, und London 1975, also Punk, entstanden waren.
Und auch ein anderes Referenzfeld der späten Achtziger Jahre-Kunst und ihrer frühen postkolonialen Agenda kam aus der Zeitgeschichte: In den sechziger und siebziger Jahren war das Interesse an anderen „Kulturen" mit deren Recht auf Selbstdarstellung von verschiedenen peripheren Gesellschaften gegen das Imperium des Westens, also generell im Rahmen einer romantischen oder ideologischen Dritte-Welt-Solidarität der europäischen Linken erstmals definiert worden. Das machte im Aufbruch der unterschiedlichen antikolonialen Kämpfe, des Vietnamkrieges und der 1968 beginnenden Krise des Westens politisch Sinn. Dennoch war die „Dritte Welt"-Kultur in gewisser Hinsicht immer ein negatives Ideal. Da dieses Konzept problematisch zu definieren war, weil die ästhetischen Kanons unhinterfragt die des westlichen Kunstbetriebes geblieben

waren, blieb davon nur der Einsatz für eine Ansammlung „nationaler Kulturen auf dem Weg zur Selbstbestimmung".
Auch in bezug auf eine dritte wichtige Dichotomie der Moderne, nämlich der Bedeutung des Zeit-Raum-Verhältnisses in der Ontologie der Kunst, hatte sich die Postmoderne mit ihren Diskursen über Architektur und Stadt von den hochmodernen Diskursen über Poesie und Musik abgelöst – auf welche sich etwa Adornos Text ja noch bezieht. Die Poetische Sprache, die Neue Musik und ihr ästhetischer Autonomieanspruch, welche Schaubeispiel für die anderen Künste gewesen waren – sie inspirierten zum Beispiel ja auch Clement Greenbergs paradigmatische Theorie der Malerei – verschwanden aus den theoretischen Texten zur Kunst zusehends als Referenz. Die Rede von der Zeit als dem dominierenden Faktor der Moderne und des Modernismus und vom Raum als jenem der Postmoderne, bedeutete etwas sowohl Thematisches als auch Empirisches. Adorno hatte in seinem Text noch einmal, ohne dezidiert darauf hinzuweisen, auch jenes diskursive Feld der bürgerlichen Philosophie Anfang des letzten Jahrhunderts, in dem die älteren Fraktionen der Neo-Kantianer, der Idealisten, der Evolutionisten und Vitalisten ihre Kämpfe gegen die jungen Phänomenologen, logischen Positivisten, Sprachphilosophen ausfochten, evoziert.

Von heute aus scheint es keine therapeutische Möglichkeit mehr zu geben, die Verdrängungsgeschichten der frühen neunziger Jahre im Sinne einer historischen Wahrheit aufzuarbeiten. Aber man kann auf einige Motive, die in dieser Verdrängungsarbeit am Werk waren, hinweisen. Dann lassen sich die kritischen KünstlerInnen der neunziger Jahre möglicherweise als künstlerisch Handelnde beschreiben, ihre Arbeit läßt sich als ein Spur gewordener Effekt beschreiben, als ein nicht auf eine Erzählung reduzierbares heterogenes System technologischer, diskursiver, kultureller, sozialer und anderer Referenzen sowie Praktiken erkennen. Und als so etwas wie das Markieren einer Ruptur, eines Einbruchs von Diskontinuitäten sowohl in die Beziehungen innerhalb eines künstlerischen Feldes wie in den Kontext eines nahezu petrifiziert scheinenden Feldes des Sprechens und Schreibens über Kunst.
Das Problem bei dieser Rekonstruktionsarbeit ist allein nicht die exekutive Macht des Kunstbetriebes gegenüber seinen PartizipantInnen, die die Archive bestimmt

und verzerrt, sie ist nicht abstrakt etwas „Falsches“, sondern es ist die Normalisierung und „Legalisierung“ bestimmter Strategien des Diskurses und der Repräsentation selbst.

Der Gestus vieler Werke, die Ende der achtziger und Anfang der neunziger Jahre im Zusammenhang von Neo-Konzept, kritischer Medienkunst oder politischer Informationsdisplays sowie von Arbeiten mit emanzipativen Bezügen auf Pop und alternative Praxen entstanden waren, aber auch von Praxen im Feld situativer Installation oder site-spezifischer Intervention im öffentlichen Raum, war oft selbst tief in einem Denken der Moderne über die Gesellschaft als einer Disziplinierungsgesellschaft verhaftet. Oder er ging zumindest von einem disziplinierenden Konzept des Raumes aus, das in seiner Adaption von Konzepten der sechziger und siebziger Jahre schon historisch geworden war. Zum anderen aber leuchtete gerade in dieser Historizität, diesem Abgeschlossen-Wirken ein Moment der Utopie auf, das gegen die Normalisierungsstrategien des Kunstbetriebes scharf gemacht werden könnte: daß es nach wie vor möglich war, ein distantes, ja ein pädagogisches Verhältnis zu den Symbolsystemen dieses Betriebes zu entwickeln, um in einem neuen, selbstbestimmteren Raum produzieren zu können. Ich glaube, letzteres war – neben den Solidarisierungsinstanzen einer um neue Beats und Klänge sich bewegenden Szenenkultur – wohl einer der Hauptgründe für die Selbstwahrnehmung vieler sehr disparater und über den Kontinent verstreut lokal Agierender als vernetztes Feld mit gemeinsamen Handlungsräumen, die sich in Opposition zu den Institutionen des Betriebes und Marktes entwickelten.

Die Solidarisierung aus institutionalisierter Rivalenschaft zum Betrieb wurde gegen Ende der Dekade dann ja oft abgelöst von einer sentimentalen Solidarität der historisch Alliierten eines Feldes, und von einer Art retrospektiven Romantisierung seiner Zustände. Die Tage, als man gegen den gemeinsamen Gegner vereint war, wurden sozusagen idealisiert und heroisiert.

Von heute aus gesehen mag es deshalb ebenso fragwürdig wie manieriert erscheinen, wenn eine Gruppe von KünstlerInnen in ihrer Selbstdarstellung sich explizit auf solche Momente der historischen und vor-postmodernen Kritik an der Moderne berief, die anderswo kaum in das kulturelle Leben der frühen neunziger Jahre eingeschrieben waren. Vor dem kulturellen Klima dieser Jahre allerdings wird klar, daß es hier darum

[03] Ebd., S. 64.

ging, die Codes von Kunstpraxen vorzuführen, die ausgezogen waren, die klassischen Oppositionen des Gewöhnlichen gegen das Elaborierte, des Alltäglichen gegen das Sublime aufzulösen und die Opposition von Politik und Kunst in eine Produktionsweise der Politik der Kunst zu transferieren.
Schon in den internen Diskussionen der ProponentInnen zeigte sich jedoch bald die potentiell ikonoklastische Kraft des Feldes: Das Projekt der Kritik an der Postmoderne mit Rückgriff auf die Kritik der Moderne aus den sechziger Jahren ließ sich auch deshalb so leicht in den Kanon der neunziger Jahre einbringen, weil es die Voraussetzungen der Möglichkeiten von Kommunikation als solche definiert hatte – als Möglichkeiten, die in den disziplinierenden Raumfiguren und Konzepten der Moderne selbst als Autonomieversprechen aufgehoben sind.
„In die Idee geistiger Produktion selbst ist ein Giftstoff geraten. Ihr Selbstbewußtsein, das Vertrauen Geschichte zu machen, ist ausgehöhlt. Dazu stimmt, daß sie, gerade auch insofern sie rezipiert wird, nicht mehr eingreift. Selbst ihre exponiertesten Äußerungen sind nicht mehr sicher vor dem integralen Kulturbetrieb.“ [03]
Ähnlich wie das Adorno hier in bezug auf die Trivialisierung und populäre Stilisierung der Kunst des Jahrhundertbeginns in der Kulturbetriebsamkeit der zwanziger Jahre beschreibt, wurde die Kunst des Anfangs der neunziger Jahre von ihrer Rezeption überschrieben, institutionell verfügbar und integrierbar gemacht: Reduktion von Information und Kontextreduzierung mit dem Ziel, die Arbeit so homogen wie möglich zu machen, den Handlungsraum von Künstler sowie BetrachterInnen streng durch ein identifizierbares Set von Objekten und Bewegungsmöglichkeiten kontrollierbar zu halten sowie durch die Parallelisierung von Motiven der Modernekritik mit einer konsumistisch-designorientierten Affirmation der Formwelten des Modernismus der sechziger und siebziger Jahre ein stilistisch und nicht inhaltistisch zuordenbares Feld zu konstruieren und zu etablieren.

In und gegen Institutionen zu arbeiten, erforderte, den Widerspruch gegen die Institutionalisierung von Absichten, die die Macht dieser Institutionen reproduzieren, zu akzeptieren. Institutionalisiert zu werden hingegen heißt, die Bedürfnisse der Institutionen auf ihrer Suche nach neuen, diskreteren oder direkteren Formen der Verlängerung ihrer

4 Ebd.

Stellung zu befriedigen. Ich glaube, daß das einer der Hauptwidersprüche der ersten Hälfte der neunziger Jahre war: Der Konflikt zwischen dem Anspruch auf Kritik und dem Bewußtsein der spezialisierten Aufgabe und Rolle des einzelnen Künstlers innerhalb des Gefüges des Betriebes, das die Kritik adressierte, war in bezug auf den Status von Autorenschaft und Autonomie nicht ausreichend reflektiert.

In einer Figur wie der Adornos, mit ihrem elitistischen Beharren auf der Position der Autorschaft, auf einem essentiellen, unveräußerlichen Rest von Subjektivität, von Identität, diesem zutiefst zwiespältigen Verharren auf den Residuen einer idealistischen, bürgerlichen Künstlerrolle, die man auch als naiven liberal-humanistischen Universalismus sehen kann, in dieser Festschreibung eines Restes erhalten sich aber auch Widerstandspotentiale gegenüber einer sozialen Realität der institutionellen Machtstrukturen, die diesen Rest entmündigen wollen.

Also bliebe auch in bezug auf den Aufbruch der frühen neunziger Jahre mit Adorno zu sagen: „Die Tradition, auch die antitraditionelle, ist abgebrochen, halbvergessene Aufgaben sind zurückgeblieben. (...) Impulse wären aufzunehmen, die schon in jenen Jahren zu erstarren drohten oder verpufften.“ [04] Der Erfolg der Epochenkunstgeschichte gründet jedenfalls im Fall der neunziger Jahre nicht nur darauf, daß in ihr hegemoniale Verhältnisse oft als das kulturelle Klima der Zeit dargestellt werden, beziehungsweise als ihre stil- und ideengeschichtliche Natur beschrieben werden. Ihr Erfolg gründet auch darauf, ob es ihr gelingt – unter Unterschlagung der politischen Natur des Symbolischen selbst – eine auf einen markenhaften Kern hin zurechtredigierte „Ausdrucksform“ der Epoche oszillieren zu lassen.

Adorno ging es in seiner Kritik der zwanziger Jahre nicht nur um biographische Sentimentalität und die Verteidigung seines eigenen Werteimperiums gegen dessen Vereinnahmung von dem, was er Kulturindustrie zu nennen gewohnt war. Es ging ihm um mehr, nämlich um die seinem Schreiben etwa über Musik ja ständig inhärenten Fragen, welchen spezifischen Raum die Repräsentationen von Kunst erzeugen können, welche Eindeutigkeit möglich ist, die sich auf der Widersprüchlichkeit des Ästhetischen und seiner Analyse als Produktionsweise gründet. Das sind bis heute auch für die Kunst jener neunziger Jahre wichtige, wenngleich weitgehend unbeantwortete Fragen geblieben.

AUTOREN

Isabelle Graw

studierte politische Wissenschaft in Paris, ist Kunstkritikerin und lebt in Berlin. Sie veröffentlichte zahlreiche Texte in Kunstzeitschriften und ist Professorin für Kunsttheorie an der Städelschule in Frankfurt am Main. Veröffentlichungen (Auswahl): *Silberblick. Texte zu Kunst und Politik* (Berlin 1999), *Die bessere Hälfte. Künstlerinnen im 20. und 21. Jahrhhundert* (Köln 2003).

Georg Schöllhammer

ist leitender Redakteur von *springerin – Hefte für Gegenwartskunst.*

ABBILDUNGEN / VERZEICHNIS DER AUSGESTELLTEN ARBEITEN

Florian Pumhösl

* Village, Museum, 2002
University of Dar Es Salaam, Library
C-Print auf DIFO, 45 x 30 cm
Courtesy Galerie Krobath Wimmer, Wien

* Village, Museum, 2002
University of Dar Es Salaam, Housing Units
C-Print auf DIFO, 45 x 30 cm
Courtesy Galerie Krobath Wimmer, Wien
(ohne Abb.)

* Village, Museum, 2002
Ceramics Factory, Dodoma
C-Print auf DIFO, 45 x 30 cm
Courtesy Galerie Krobath Wimmer, Wien
(ohne Abb.)

Isa Genzken

* Ohne Titel (Weltempfänger), o.J.
Beton, Metall, 30 x 43,3 x 8,5 cm
Courtesy Galerie Daniel Buchholz, Köln
(ohne Abb.)

* „Rudolf" (Weltempfänger), 1990
Beton, Metall, 72 x 44,5 x 9,5 cm
Courtesy Galerie Daniel Buchholz, Köln
(ohne Abb.)

* Ohne Titel (Weltempfänger), 1999
Beton, Metall, 36 x 24 x 7,6 cm
Courtesy Galerie Daniel Buchholz, Köln
(ohne Abb.)

Weltempfänger, 1988-89
Beton, Metall
Verschiedene Größen
Installationsansicht
Courtesy Galerie Daniel Buchholz, Köln
(Abb.)

Weltempfänger, 1992
Beton, Metall, 10 x 30 x 5 cm
Courtesy Galerie Daniel Buchholz, Köln
(Abb.)

Sarah Morris

* Library of Congress [Capital], 2001
Lack auf Leinwand, 214 x 214 x 5 cm
Sammlung Goetz
Foto: Courtesy Sammlung Goetz
Stephen White

* Worldbank [Capital], 2001
Lack auf Leinwand, 152,5 x 152,5 cm
Sammlung Goetz
Foto: Courtesy White Cube, London
Stephen White

Art & Language

* Untitled Painting, 1965
Spiegel auf Leinwand montiert
2 Teile, je 119,3 x 58,3 x 10,9 cm
Courtesy Lisson Gallery, London
Foto: Stephen White, London

Secret Painting, 1967-68
Acryl auf Leinwand und Photostat
2 Teile, je 97 x 97 each
Courtesy Lisson Gallery, London
Foto: Gareth Winters

Andre Cadere

* Barre de bois ronde
Bemaltes Holz, 198 x 2 cm
Collection FRAC Nord - Pas de Calais, Dunkerque
Foto: E. Watteau

Thomas Demand

* Simulator, 2003
C-Print/Diasec, 465 x 330 cm
Courtesy Schipper & Krome, Berlin
(Abbildung: Arbeitsfotos)

Carl Andre

* Aluminium-Steel Dipole (E/W), 1973
2 Einheiten, Seite an Seite
Aluminium Osten, Stahl Westen
0,5 x 100 x 100 cm
Sammlung Osarek, Berlin

Samuel Beckett

* Quad I & II (Quadrat I & II)
entstanden 1981, Erstsendung 1982
Quad I: 15 Min.
Quad II: 5 Min.
Courtesy Éditions De Minuit, Paris
©Südwestrundfunk Stuttgart

Peter Friedl

* Ohne Titel (badly organized), 2003
Glasbuchstaben, Neon
70 x 260 x 6 cm

Christopher Williams

* Model: 1964 Renault Dauphine-Four, R-1095
Body Type & Seating: 4-dr-sedan- 4 to 5 persons
Engine Type: 14/52 Weight: 1397 lbs
Price $ 1495,00 USD (original)
ENGINE DATA:

Base four: inline, overhead-valve four cylinder
Cast iron block and aluminium head W/removable cylinder sleeves. Displacement: 51.5 cu.in (845 oc.)
Bore and stroke: 2.28 x 3.15 in (58 x 80 mm) Compression Ratio: 7.25 : 1 Brake Horsepower: 32 (SAE) at 4200 rpm
Torque: 50 lbs. At 2000 rpm,
Three main bearings. Solid valve lifters
Single downdraft carburetor
CHASSIS DATA:
Wheelbase: 89 in. Overall length: 155 in. Heigth: 57 in. Width: 60 in. Front thread: 49 in. Rear thread: 48 in.
Standard Tires: 5.50 x 15 in.
TECHNICAL:
Layout: rear engine, rear drive. Transmission: four speed manual
Stearing: rack and pinion. Suspension (front): independent coil springs
Brakes: front/rear disc. Body construction: steel unibody
PRODUCTION DATA:
Sales: 18,432 sold in the U.S. in 1964 (all types)
Manufacturer: Regie Nationale des Usines Renault, Billancourt, France
Distributor: Renault Inc., New York, NY, U.S.A.

Serial number: R-10950059799
Engine number: Type 670-05 # 191 563
California License Plate number: UOU 087
Vehicle ID Number: 0059799
January 15, 2000 (Nr. 9) 2000
Gelatin silver print
64,5 x 74,5 cm
Editions of 10
Wilhelm und Gaby Schürmann

Stephen Prina

An Evening of 19th and 20th Century Piano Music, LACE, Los Angeles 1986 (Plakat)

An Evening of 19th and 20th Century Piano Music, Museum of Contemporary Art, Los Angeles 1988 (Programmheft)

An Evening of 19th and 20th Century Piano Music, Museum of Contemporary Art, Los Angeles 1988 (Einladungskarte)
Courtesy Gisela Capitain, Köln

Mathias Poledna

* Western Recording, 2003
16mm-Film
10:30 Min.
Courtesy Richard Telles Fine Art,

Los Angeles und
Galerie Meyer Kainer, Wien

Gerhard Richter

* Grau, 1976
Öl auf Leinwand
200 x 200 cm
Privatsammlung
Foto: Rudolf Nagel

Jonathan Monk

* High School Boogie-Woogie, 2002
16mm Film, Loop
Würfelgröße: 5,7 cm
Collection of Nell and Jack Wendler, London
Courtesy Casey Kaplan, New York
Foto: Dave Morgan

* Sol LeWitt's Twenty First Sentence on Conceptual Art: From One Restaurant To The Next (Frankfurt am Main), 2003
24-teilige Papierarbeit
Courtesy Meyer Riegger Galerie, Karlsruhe (ohne Abb.)

Ad Reinhardt

* Bild Nr. 16, 1955
Öl auf Leinwand, 203,5 x 101,5 cm
Museum Wiesbaden, Dauerleihgabe des Museumsvereins Otto Ritschl e.V.
Foto: Ed Restle

Andreas Slominski

* Ohne Titel, 1987
Stoff, 10 x 20 x 19 cm
Museum für Moderne Kunst, Frankfurt am Main
Erworben mit privaten Mitteln als Dauerleihgabe für das Museum für Moderne Kunst, Frankfurt am Main
Foto: Rudolf Nagel

Ohne Titel, 1990
* Pappe, Papier, Leinen
78,3 x 55,4 cm
Museum für Moderne Kunst, Frankfurt am Main
Foto: Rudolf Nagel

Martin Boyce

* Untitled (After Rietveld), 1999
Neonröhren, Stahlband
183 x 183 x 183 cm
Sammlung Haubrok

oto ©Martin Boyce and The Modern
nstitute, Glasgow

ason Dodge

Why are you afraid of distances, 2003
luminium, Kabel
Maße variabel
Courtesy Casey Kaplan, New York

Maria Eichhorn

6 Kästen Mineralwasser (SPA) /
Gläser, 1995
ammlung Anja Lohmüller
Courtesy Galerie Barbara Weiss
oto: Jens Ziehe

Martin Creed

The lights going on and off
Work No. 127, 1995
Maße variabel
Courtesy Johnen + Schöttle, Köln
ohne Abb.)

Work No. 270
The lights off, 2001
nstallationsansicht Johnen + Schöttle,
Köln (Abb.)

Liam Gillick

* Discussion Island Reconciliation
Plates, 1997
4 Aluminiumbleche, Schrauben, gewölbte
Schraubenkopfverblendungen
100 x 200 cm
Courtesy Schipper & Krome, Berlin
(ohne Abb.)

(The What If? Scenario) Mirrored
Insulation Plate, 1996
Aluminiumblech, Schrauben, gewölbte
Schraubenkopfverblendungen
100 x 200 cm
Courtesy Schipper & Krome, Berlin (Abb.)

Cerith Wyn Evans

* Adorno Centenary („The Stars Down
to Earth“ published 1974), 2003
Artemide Lampe (Miconos Sospensione),
Flatscreen, Morse Code Unit, Computer
Maße variabel
Courtesy Galerie Daniel Buchholz, Köln
(ohne Abb.)

Cleave 02 (The Accursed Share), 2002
Laptop, Blende, Pflanzen, Text von
George Bataille
Maße variabel
Courtesy White Cube, London (Abb.)

Henrik Plenge Jakobsen

* Kapital Melankolie (Prismatisch), 2003
Runde Sägeblätter, optisches Glas, Schrauben
35 x 35 x 6 cm
Courtesy Galleri Nicolai Wallner, Kopenhagen

* Kapital Melankolie (Chromatisch), 2003
Vinylschallplatte, Fluorit, Schrauben
30 x 30 x 5 cm
Courtesy Galleri Nicolai Wallner, Kopenhagen

* Kapital Melankolie (Zwölfton), 2003
Plattenspieler, rundes Sägeblatt, Fluorit
10 x 33 x 44 cm
Courtesy Galleri Nicolai Wallner, Kopenhagen

Christopher Williams

* Model: 1964 Renault Dauphine-Four, R-1095
Body Type & Seating: 4-dr-sedan- 4 to 5 persons
Engine Type: 14/52 Weight: 1397 lbs
Price $ 1495,00 USD (original)
ENGINE DATA:
Base four: inline, overhead-valve four cylinder
Cast iron block and aluminium head W/removable cylinder sleeves. Displacement: 51.5 cu.in (845 oc.)
Bore and stroke: 2.28 x 3.15 in (58 x 80 mm) Compression
Ratio: 7.25 : 1 Brake Horsepower: 32 (SAE) at 4200 rpm
Torque: 50 lbs. At 2000 rpm, Three main bearings. Solid valve lifters
Single downdraft carburetor
CHASSIS DATA:
Wheelbase: 89 in. Overall length: 155 in
Heigth: 57 in. Width: 60 in. Front thread: 49 in. Rear thread: 48 in.
Standard Tires: 5.50 x 15 in.
TECHNICAL:
Layout: rear engine, rear drive. Transmission: four speed manual
Stearing: rack and pinion. Suspension (front): independent coil springs
Brakes: front/rear disc. Body construction: steel unibody
PRODUCTION DATA:
Sales: 18,432 sold in the U.S. in 1964 (all types)
Manufacturer: Regie Nationale des Usines Renault, Billancourt, France
Distributor: Renault Inc., New York, NY, U.S.A

erial number: R-10950059799
ngine number: Type 670-05 # 191 563
alifornia License Plate number: UOU 087
ehicle ID Number: 0059799
anuary 15, 2000 (Nr. 10) 2000
elatin silver print
4,5 x 74,5 cm
ditions of 10
Vilhelm und Gaby Schürmann

uan Macdonald

Poor Blumfeld, 2002
DVDs, 2 Monitore
ourtesy Cohan and Leslie, New York
nd Zink & Gegner, München

irsten Pieroth

Postkarten aus Berlin, 2002
5 Postkarten, 45 Computerprints
eweils 10 x 14,8 cm
ourtesy Klosterfelde, Berlin
ohne Abb.)

rief nach Berlin, 2003
rief nach Berlin, der am 29. April 2003
n einen deutschen Briefkasten im
ostmuseum in Kairo eingeworfen wurde.
ourtesy Klosterfelde, Berlin (Abb.)

Mein Flug über den Ozean, 2002
Lindberg Buch, Briefmarken, Kordel
4,5 x 20,8 x 14 cm
Courtesy De Chiara Gallery, New York
(Abb.)

Gustav Metzger

* Modell eines auto-destruktiven Monuments, 1960 (Rekonstruktion 1997)
33 x 14,5 x 12 cm
Besitz des Künstlers

* Auto-destructive Art, 1959/60
Manifest
Besitz des Künstlers (ohne Abb.)

Lawrence Weiner

* MISCELLANOUS OBJECTS (MADE BY HAND) GIVEN TO THE TIDE FOR A TIME, 1989
Schrift auf Wand
Sammlung Osarek, Potsdam

Louise Lawler

* Untitled (Collection of 60 Drawings), 1992-93
Cibachrome, Filz, Kristall
Höhe: 5,08 cm, Durchmesser: 8,89 cm
Courtesy Monika Sprüth Philomene Magers, Köln

* Untitled (Attachments), 1993
Cibachrome, Filz, Kristall
Höhe: 5,08 cm, Durchmesser: 8,89 cm
Courtesy Monika Sprüth Philomene Magers, Köln

Bruce Nauman

* Concrete Tape Recorder Piece, 1968
Beton, Tonbandrekorder, Tonbandrolle
30,5 x 61 x 61 cm
Flick Collection
Foto: A. Burger, Zürich

John Massey

* As the Hammer Strikes (A Partial Illustration), 1982
3 Kanal synchronisierte DVD Installation
30 Minuten (Rekonstruktion der 16mm Filminstallation)
National Gallery of Canada, Ottawa

Markus Schinwald

* Adornorama, 2003
25 x 25 x 25 cm
Courtesy Georg Kargl, Wien

Christopher Williams

* Model: 1964 Renault Dauphine-Four, R-1095
Body Type & Seating: 4-dr-sedan- 4 to 5 persons
Engine Type: 14/52 Weight: 1397 lbs
Price $ 1495,00 USD (original)
ENGINE DATA:
Base four: inline, overhead-valve four cylinder
Cast iron block and aluminium head W/removable cylinder sleeves. Displacement: 51.5 cu.in (845 oc.)
Bore and stroke: 2.28 x 3.15 in (58 x 80 mm) Compression Ratio: 7.25 : 1 Brake Horsepower: 32 (SAE) at 4200 rpm
Torque: 50 lbs. At 2000 rpm,
Three main bearings. Solid valve lifters
Single downdraft carburetor
CHASSIS DATA:
Wheelbase: 89 in. Overall length: 155 in
Heigth: 57 in. Width: 60 in. Front thread: 49 in. Rear thread: 48 in.
Standard Tires: 5.50 x 15 in.

TECHNICAL:
Layout: rear engine, rear drive. Transmission: four speed manual
Steering: rack and pinion. Suspension (front): independent coil springs
Brakes: front/rear disc.
Body construction: steel unibody
PRODUCTION DATA:
Sales: 18,432 sold in the U.S. in 1964 (all types)
Manufacturer: Regie Nationale des Usines Renault, Billancourt, France
Distributor: Renault Inc., New York, NY, U.S.A.
Serial number: R-10950059799
Engine number: Type 670-05 # 191 563
California License Plate number: UOU 087
Vehicle ID Number: 0059799
January 15, 2000 (Nr. 6) 2000
Gelatin silver print
64,5 x 74,5 cm
Editions of 10
Wilhelm und Gaby Schürmann

* in der Ausstellung gezeigte Werke

DANK AN DIE LEIHGEBER:

Daniel Buchholz, Köln
Gisela Capitain, Köln
Collection FRAC Nord - Pas de Calais, Dunkerque
Flick Collection
Sammlung Goetz
Sammlung Haubrok, Düsseldorf
Johnen + Schöttle, Köln
Georg Kargel, Wien
Klosterfelde, Berlin
Krobath Wimmer, Wien
Lisson Gallery, London
Sammlung Anja Lohmüller, Berlin
Meyer Kainer, Wien
Museum für Moderne Kunst, Frankfurt am Main
Museum Wiesbaden
National Gallery of Canada, Ottawa
Sammlung Osarek, Berlin
Schipper & Krome, Berlin
Wilhelm und Gaby Schürmann, Aachen
Monika Sprüth Philomene Magers, Köln
Galleri Nicolai Wallner, Kopenhagen
White Cube, London
Zink & Gegner, München
sowie weitere Leihgeber, die ungenannt bleiben möchten.

CARL ANDRE
ART & LANGUAGE
SAMUEL BECKETT
MARTIN BOYCE
ANDRE CADERE
MARTIN CREED
THOMAS DEMAND
JASON DODGE
MARIA EICHHORN
PETER FRIEDL
ISA GENZKEN
LIAM GILLICK
HENRIK PLENGE JAKOBSEN
LOUISE LAWLER
EUAN MACDONALD
JOHN MASSEY

GUSTAV METZGER
JONATHAN MONK
SARAH MORRIS
BRUCE NAUMAN
KIRSTEN PIEROTH
MATHIAS POLEDNA
STEPHEN PRINA
FLORIAN PUMHÖSL
AD REINHARDT
GERHARD RICHTER
MARKUS SCHINWALD
ANDREAS SLOMINSKI
LAWRENCE WEINER
CHRISTOPHER WILLIAMS
CERITH WYN EVANS

FLORIAN PUMHÖSL Village, Museum, 2002 University of Dar Es Salaam

ISA GENZKEN Weltempfänger, 1988-89

ISA GENZKEN Weltempfänger, 1992

SARAH MORRIS Libary of Congress [Capital], 2001 Photo: Courtesy Sammlung Goetz, Stephen White

SARAH MORRIS Worldbank [Capital], 2001

Photo: Courtesy White Cube, Stephen White

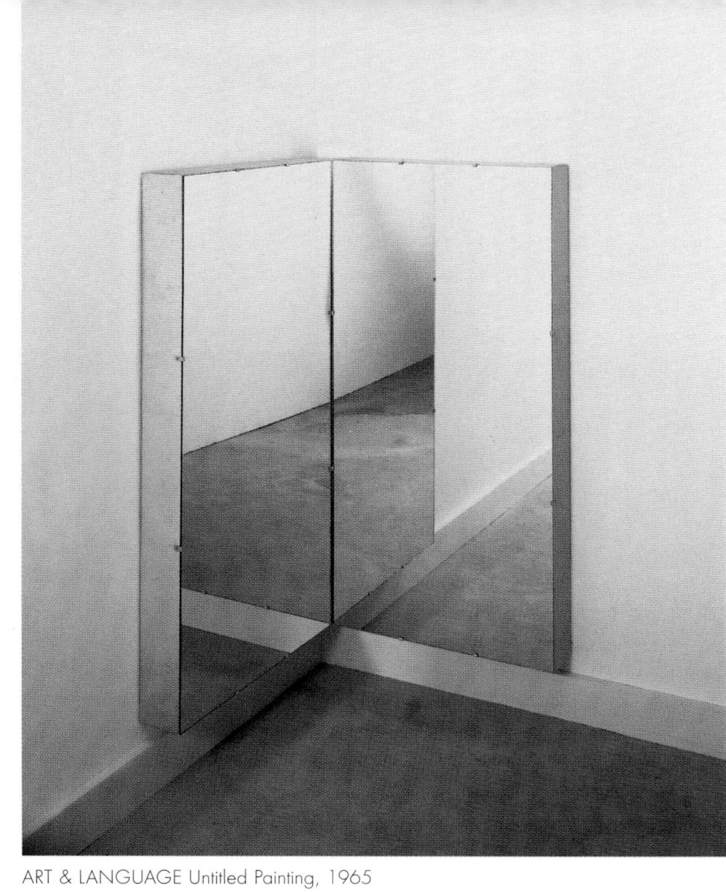

ART & LANGUAGE Untitled Painting, 1965

ART & LANGUAGE Secret Painting, 1967-68

The content of this painting is invisible; the exact character and dimension of the content are to be kept permanently secret, known only to Ian Burn.

ANDRE CADERE Barre de bois ronde

THOMAS DEMAND Simulator, 2003 (Arbeitsfotos)

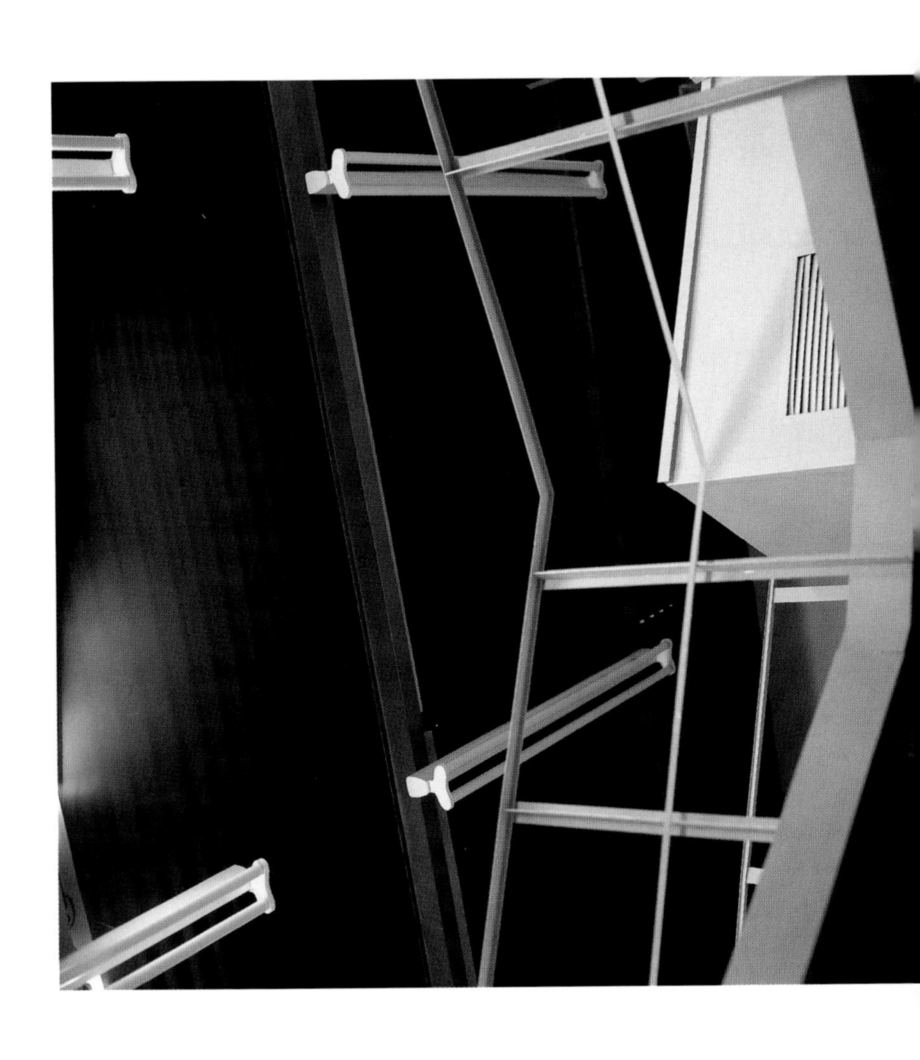

CARL ANDRE Aluminium-Steel Dipole (E/W), 1973

SAMUEL BECKETT Quad I & II (Quadrat I & II), 1981, Erstsendung 1982

In 1965 the prescience of these observations was dramatically confirmed by a series of radio lectures organized by the Deutschlandfunk on the topic **"What is German?."** Adorno's contribution, broadcast on May 9th of that year with the name of the series as its title, follows Nietzsche's lead in its critique of nationalist generalizations and its shift of emphasis to the very question itself. Indeed, when Adorno's essay is republished in 1969 it is indicative that, besides the deletion of two phrases, the only significant change is an addition to the title which now reads "Auf die Frage: 'Was ist deutsch?'." (2) The ambiguity of this query allows Adorno to develop another - quite literal - line of response: What is German? It's a language.
But such a recasting of the question of nationality as a question of language and linguistic nationality generates new problems. In order to say just what is (the) German (language), one must be able to establish the identity, limits and character of a particular language or national idiom. To do this, Adorno argues, one must take a trip to another language; a voyage, as we shall see, of translation.

Adorno's essay opens with a dialectical analysis of German national stereotypes which, despite their moment of truth, are immediately dismissed as an unproductive line of inquiry: "Ungewiß, ob es etwas wie den Deutschen, oder das Deutsche, oder irgendein Ähnliches in anderen Nationen, überhaupt gibt" (p. 691). The radicality of this claim should not be overlooked, since it effectively destroys the very foundations of traditional ontological approaches to the question "What is German?." Instead, Adorno insists on an alternative, more micrological strategy, a detour which seeks insight into the general through a careful examination of the particular. Adorno chooses as a case study his own decision to go back to Germany after years of exile in the United States and the dialectic of the foreign *[fremd]* and the native *[eigen]*, of alienation and return which was involved. This new focus is not simply autobiographical, however, since, as Adorno is careful to point out, "Auch ein Objektives machte sich geltend. Das ist die Sprache" (p. 699). While not discounting the complicated nature of his desire to return, Adorno concentrates on two linguistic experiences which really clinched the decision to leave America, both of them narratives of failed attempts at translation. (3)

Strange things happen to Adorno when moving from one language to another. He recounts how a German-speaking American publisher familiar with his *Philosophie der neuen Musik* was interested in bringing out an English-language edition and asked him to prepare a translation. Upon reading the English draft which Adorno submitted, however, the publisher suddenly discovered that the text which he earlier had so admired was **"badly organized"** (a term which appears in **"Auf die Frage: 'Was ist deutsch?'"** *in English*). Had the translation revealed something about the **"original"** or was the remark a stylistic criticism of the English rendition? If Adorno's work written in German seemed to suffer in translation, one might think that this could be avoided were Adorno to *write in English*. In the second example Adorno undertakes a symptomatic reading of the violent **"editing"** (again in English in the original) (4) done to a lecture which he had submitted to a West Coast psychoanalytic journal. (5)

In a passage from *Einbahnstraße* to which Adorno alludes in both of the *Fremdwort* essays, Walter Benjamin describes how the writer treats thought like a surgeon who, during the course of a (compositional) operation **"schiebt als silberne Rippe ein Fremdwort ein."** (13) According to Adorno's gloss, this prosthesis is necessary for the survival of the linguistic corpus *[Sprachleib]* which was dying of organic causes. In **"Auf die Frage: 'Was ist deutsch?'"** Adorno has also added four prosthetic supplements - four *Fremdwörter.* (14) Two of them - "badly organized" and "editing" - are followed by German translations, a combination which implies both that the *Fremdwort* can be translated and, since the translation is not a replacement but an addition, that it can not be. Furthermore, "badly organized" appears within quotations, marking it perhaps as a citation of the words used by the **"emigrant publisher"** who is described in a later deleted clause as **"more american than the born Americans."** The use of the English expression rather than the appropriate German words (which Adorno provides as the translation) may have struck Adorno as a repression of national difference and an instance, in the domain of language, of the adaptation which he so criticized.

The pairing of *Fremdwort* and translation stages explicitly the translative encounter (so central to Adorno's argument) which then occurs in a more veiled form in the two remaining English *Fremdwörter:* keep smiling and up to date. These appear with no indication of their foreignness and, for that reason, are all the more dangerous. What is so threatening about such unmarked linguistic aliens is conveyed in the distinction, in German, between the *Fremdwort* and the *Lehnwort* (borrowed word), the latter defined as a word of foreign origin which has become so assimilated in the course of time that its foreignness is known only to experts. (15)
The recognizable foreignness of the *Fremdwort* raises the question as to whether other words might not be *Lehnwörter,* i.e. *Fremdwörter* in disguise, and thereby casts aspersions on the **"purity"** of the most seemingly **"native"** words. The Nazis, not surprisingly, systematically eliminated the *Fremdwörter* from their literature and pedagogy from the very start. (16) In doing so they revealed very clearly, as violent resistance often does, what is at stake: the possibility of linguistic nationalism. In this light one can begin to appreciate the chilling insight of Adorno's aphoristic claim in *Minima Moralia:* "Fremdwörter," he writes, "sind die Juden der Sprache." (17)

badly organized

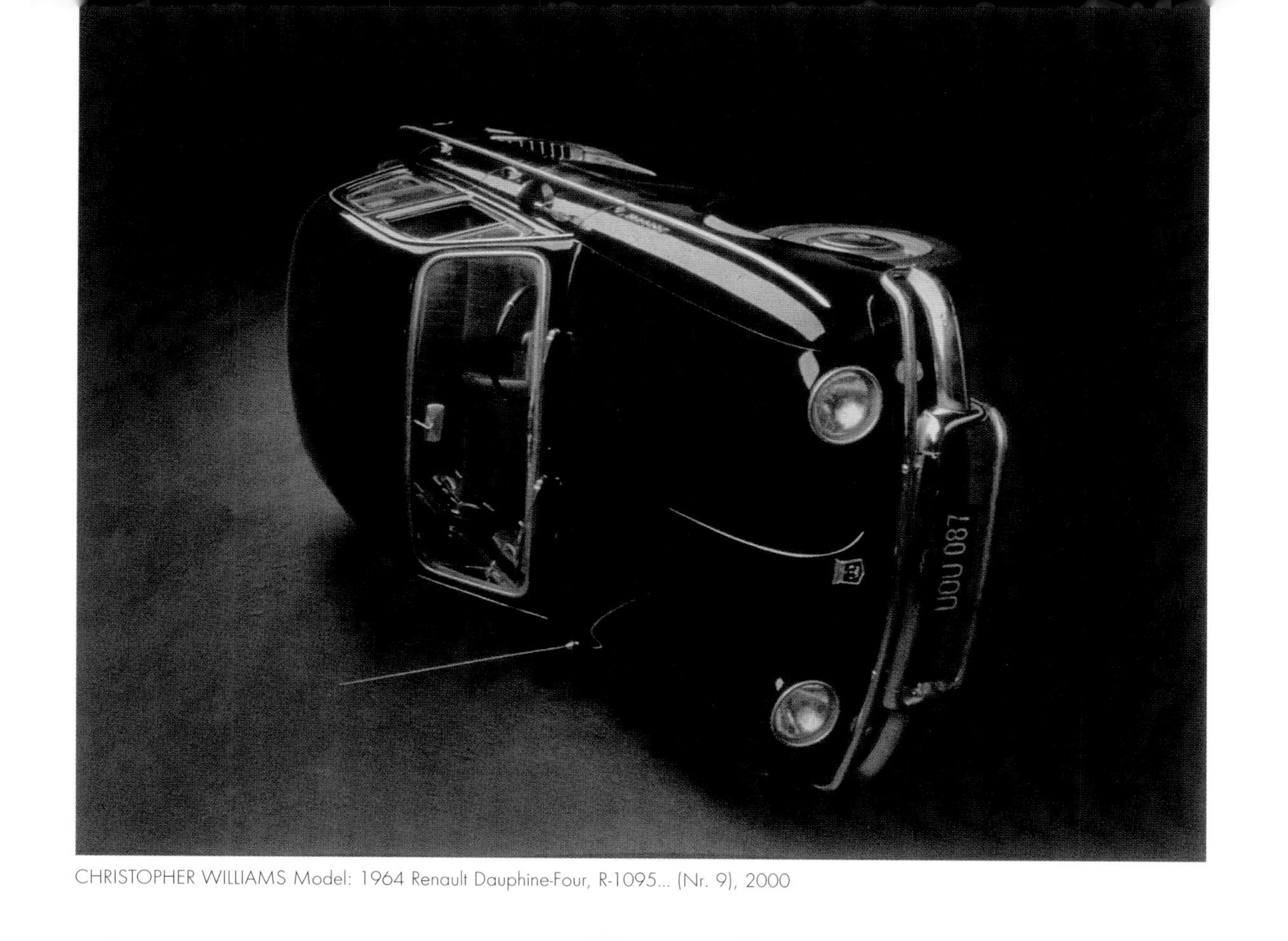

CHRISTOPHER WILLIAMS Model: 1964 Renault Dauphine-Four, R-1095... (Nr. 9), 2000

The Museum of Contemporary Art and Stephen Prina

present

AN EVENING OF 19TH- AND 20TH-CENTURY PIANO MUSIC

Excerpts from
The 9 Symphonies of
L. van Beethoven,
Für zwei Pianoforte zu vier Händen,
Transcription pour Piano à 2 mains,
and
Für Klavier zu 4 Händen,* 1983-85
Stephen Prina, arranger

Lorna Eder, piano
Gaylord Mowrey, piano

Friday, April 8, 1988, 8 p.m.
Saturday, April 9, 1988, 8 p.m.
Sunday, April 10, 1988, 2 p.m.
MOCA Ahmanson Auditorium
250 South Grand Avenue, Los Angeles
Tickets: General $6, Members, students, seniors $5
Limited seating
Information: MOCA Box Office 213/626-6828

This concert is presented as part of the exhibition "STRIKING DISTANCE," March 22-June 19, 1988, at The Temporary Contemporary. Steinway grand pianos are courtesy of Sherman-Clay. Stephen Prina also wishes to thank The Foundation for Art Resources, Los Angeles, for the generous support of the world premiere of this work at Symphony Space, New York, December 4, 1985, which was presented as part of the exhibition "The Art of Memory/The Loss of History," The New Museum of Contemporary Art, New York. *West Coast Premiere.

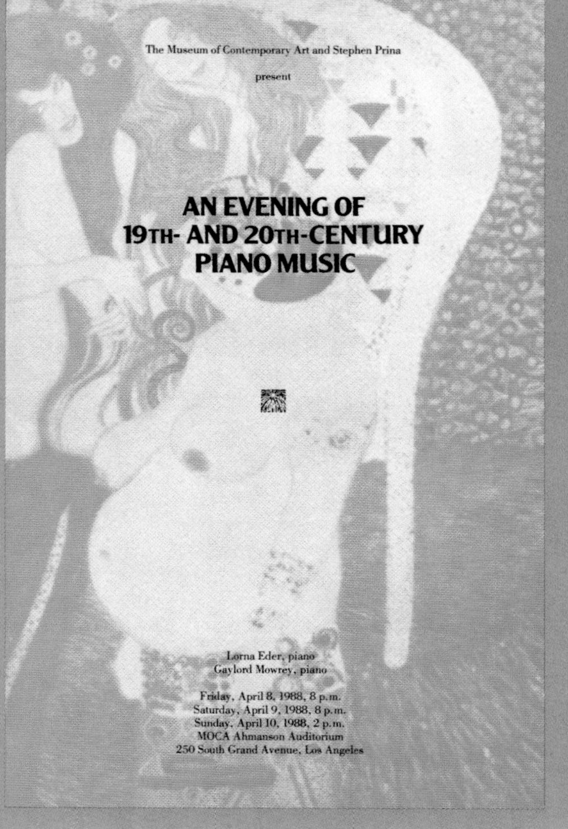

STEPHEN PRINA An Evening of 19th and 20th-Century Piano Music

The New Museum of Contemporary Art, Symphony Space and Stephen Prina
present

AN EVENING OF 19TH- AND 20TH-CENTURY PIANO MUSIC

Symphony No. 3
in E Flat Major, Op. 55,
"Eroica," 1803
L. van Beethoven
Hugo Ulrich, arranger

Excerpts from
The 9 Symphonies of
L. van Beethoven,
Für zwei Pianoforte zu vier Händen,
Transcription pour Piano à 2 mains,
and
Für Klavier zu 4 Händen, 1983-85
Stephen Prina, arranger

Trina Dye-Ballinger, piano
Gaylord Mowrey, piano

Wednesday, December 4, 1985, 8:00 p.m.
Symphony Space
2537 Broadway at 95th Street, New York, New York
Tickets: $3.00 minimum donation at the door

This concert is presented as part of the exhibition "The Art of Memory/The Loss of History," November 23, 1985–January 19, 1986, The New Museum of Contemporary Art, 583 Broadway, New York, New York. It is presented with the generous support of The Foundation for Art Resources, Los Angeles; Symphony Space; and the National Endowment for the Arts.

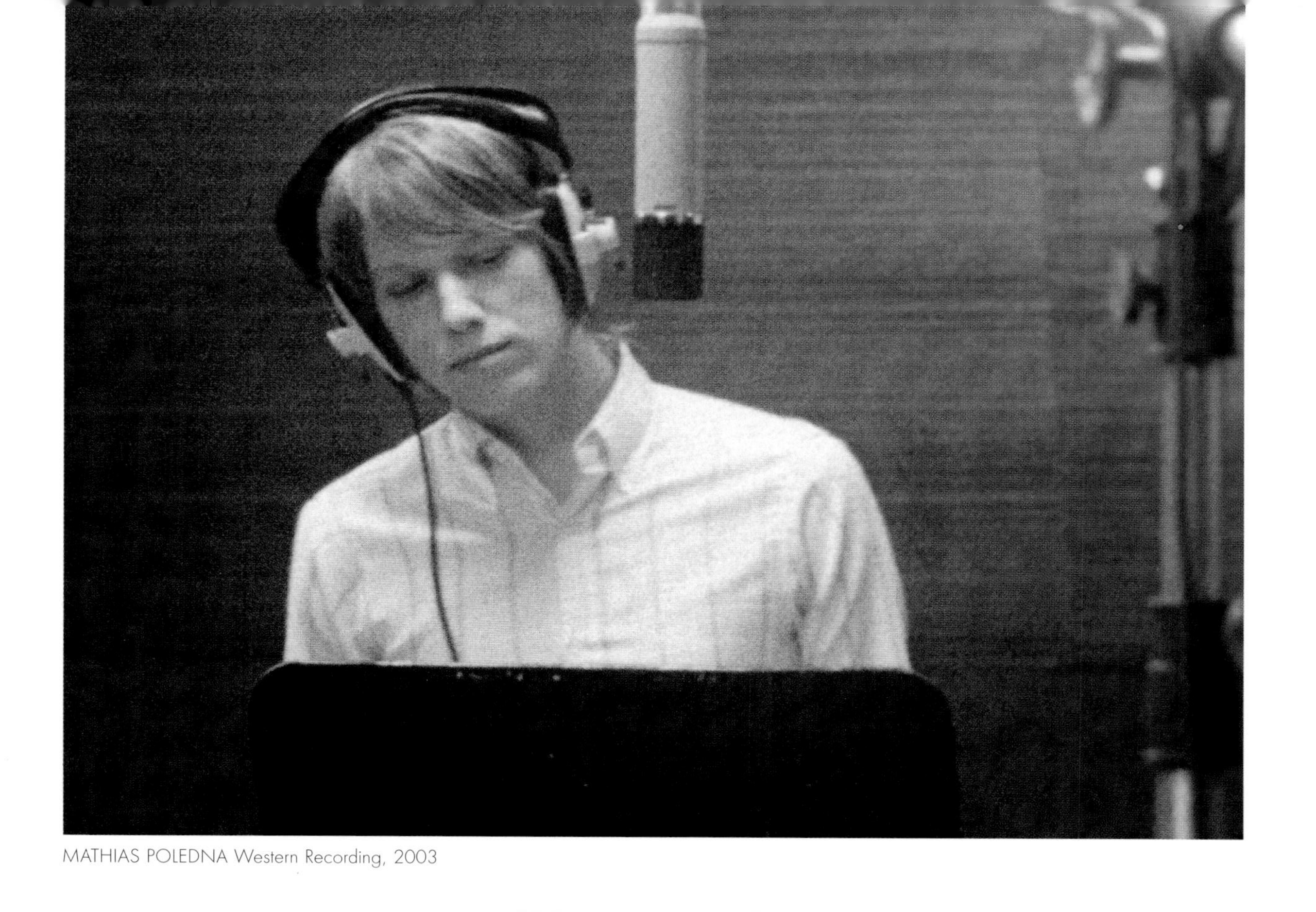

MATHIAS POLEDNA Western Recording, 2003

GERHARD RICHTER Grau, 1976

JONATHAN MONK High School Boogie-Woogie, 2002

AD REINHARDT Bild Nr. 16, 1955

ANDREAS SLOMINSKI Ohne Titel, 1987

ANDREAS SLOMINSKI Ohne Titel, 1990

MARTIN BOYCE Untitled (After Rietveld), 1999

JASON DODGE Why are you afraid of distances, 2002

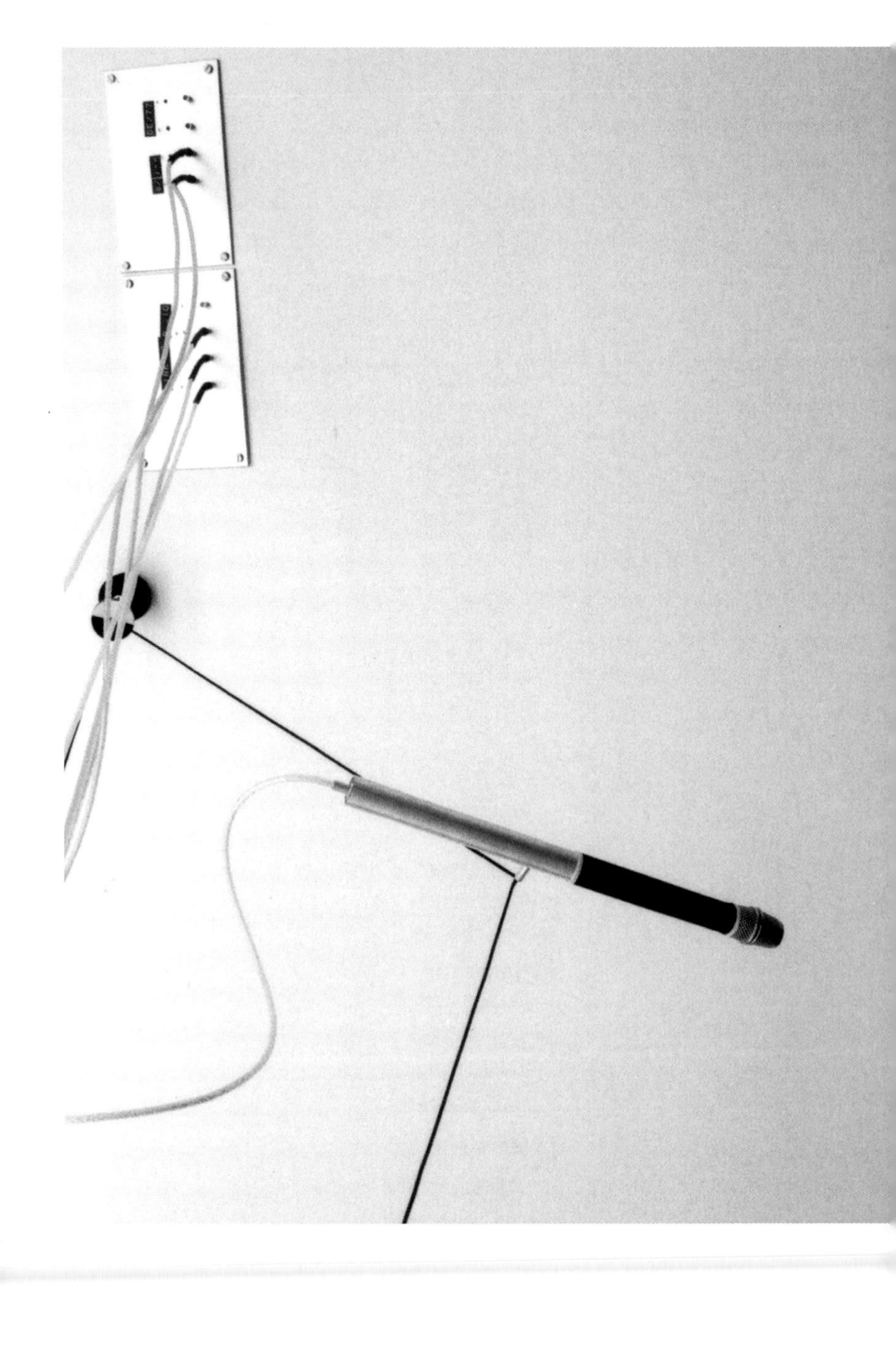

MARIA EICHHORN 6 Kästen Mineralwasser (SPA) / 7 Gläser, 1995

MARTIN CREED Work No. 270 The lights off, 2001

LIAM GILLICK (The What If? Scenario) Mirrored Insulation Plate, 1996

CERITH WYN EVANS Cleave 02 (The Accursed Share), 2002

HENRIK PLENGE JAKOBSEN Melankolie Kapital, 2003

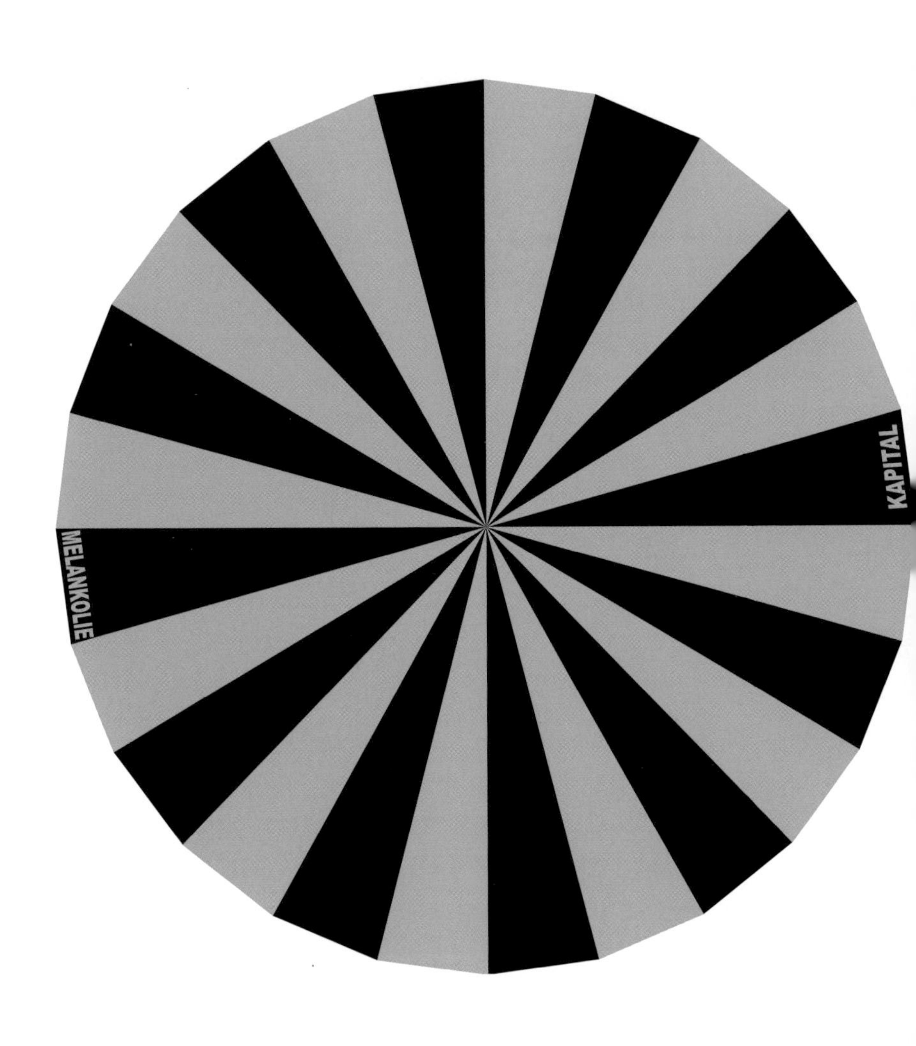
KAPITAL
MELANKOLIE

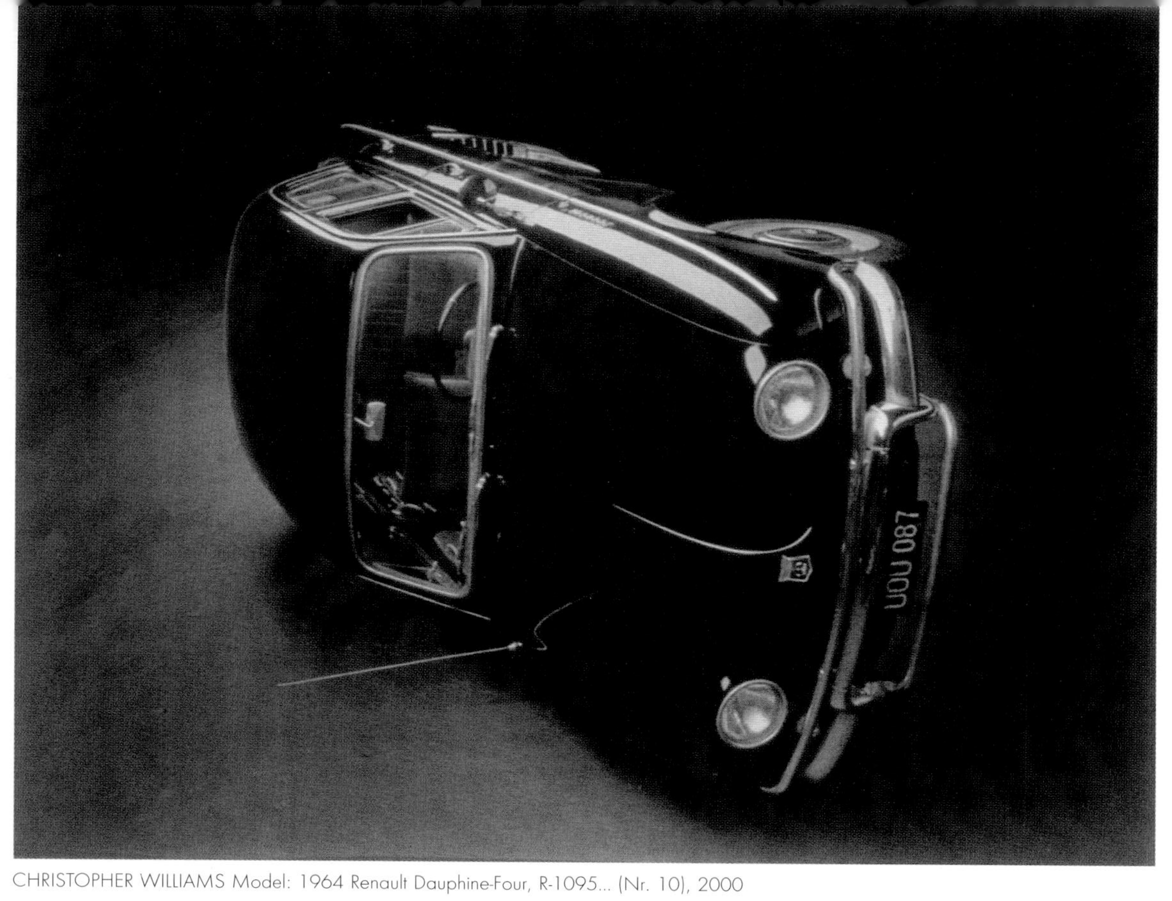

CHRISTOPHER WILLIAMS Model: 1964 Renault Dauphine-Four, R-1095... (Nr. 10), 2000

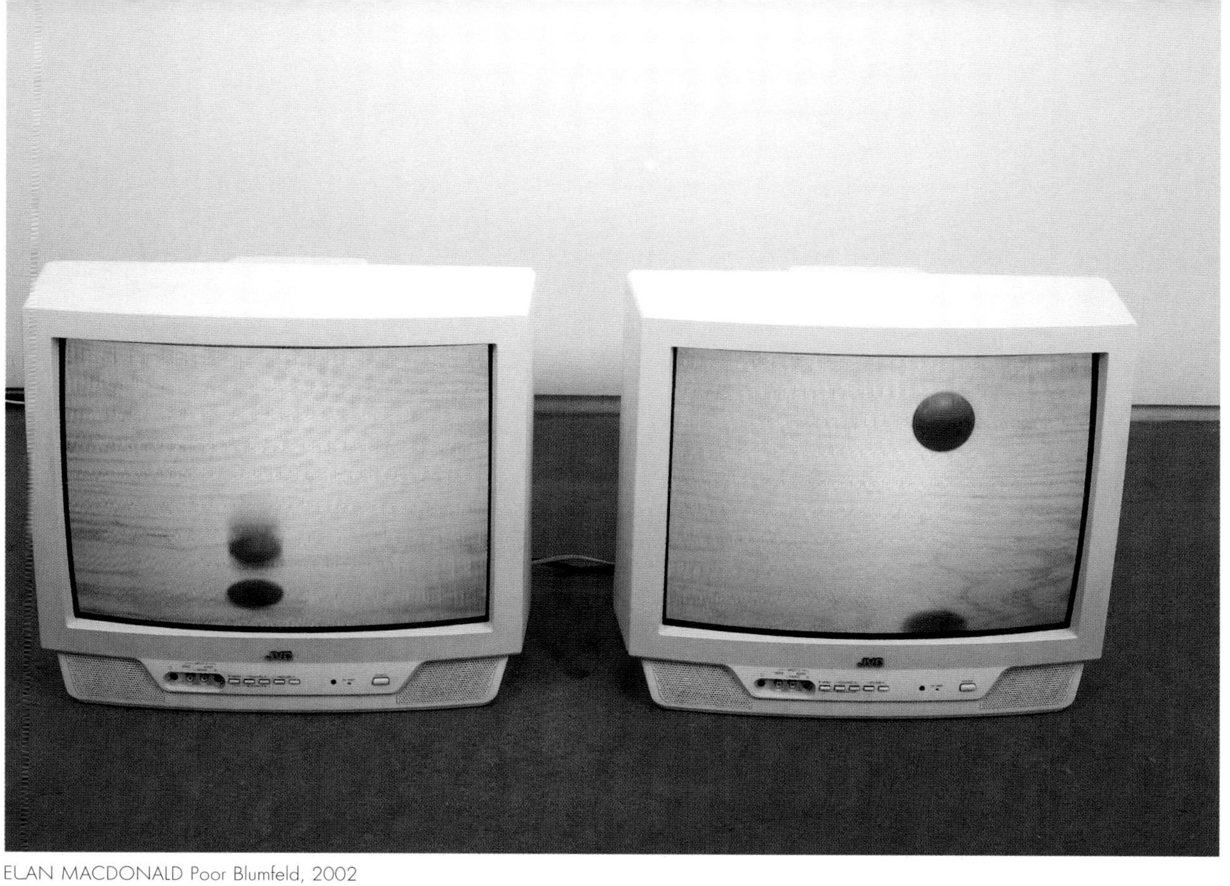

ELAN MACDONALD Poor Blumfeld, 2002